# RICH BROTT

# ACTIVATING
## Your Personal
# FAITH
## To RECEIVE

*25* Biblical Principles for
Releasing the Power Within!

# Published by ABC Book Publishing

**AbcBookPublishing.com**
Printed in U.S.A.

**Activating Your Personal Faith to Receive**
*25 Biblical Principles for Releasing the Power Within!*

10 Digit ISBN: 1-60185-008-5
13 Digit ISBN (EAN): 978-1-60185-008-9

**First Edition, January 1, 2008**
Richard A. Brott
All Rights Reserved

## About the Author

Rich Brott holds a Bachelor of Science degree in Business and Economics and a Master of Business Administration.

Rich has served in an executive position of some very successful businesses. He has functioned on the board of directors for churches, businesses, and charities and served on a college advisory board. Rich has traveled to more than 25 countries on teaching assignments and business concerns.

Rich Brott has over authored thirty-five books including:

- 5 Simple Keys to Financial Freedom
- 10 Life-Changing Attitudes That Will Make You a Financial Success
- 15 Biblical Responsibilities Leading to Financial Wisdom
- 30 Biblical Principles for Managing Your Money
- 35 Keys to Financial Independence
- A Biblical Perspective on Giving Generously
- A Biblical Perspective on Tithing & Giving
- A Biblical Perspective on Tithing Faithfully
- Achieving Financial Alignment
- Activating Your Personal Faith to Receive
- Advancing a Successful Business
- All the Financial Scriptures in the Bible
- Basic Principles for Maximizing Your Personal Cash Flow
- Basic Principles of Conservative Investing
- Biblical Principles for Achieving Personal Success

- Biblical Principles for Becoming Debt Free
- Biblical Principles for Building a Successful Business
- Biblical Principles for Financial Success - Student Workbook
- Biblical Principles for Financial Success - Teacher Workbook
- Biblical Principles for Personal Evangelism
- Biblical Principles for Releasing Financial Provision
- Biblical Principles for Staying Out of Debt
- Biblical Principles for Success in Personal Finance
- Biblical Principles That Create Success Through Productivity
- Business, Occupations, Professions & Vocations In the Bible
- Developing a Successful Personal and Business Vision
- Establishing a Successful Business
- Family Finance Handbook
- Family Finance Student Workbook
- Family Finance Teacher Workbook
- How to Receive Prosperity and Provision
- Maximizing Your Business Success
- Prosperity Has a Purpose
- Public Relations for the Local Church
- Successful Time Management

He and his wife Karen, have been married for 36 years. Rich Brott resides in Portland, Oregon, with his wife, three children, son-in-law and granddaughter.

## Dedication

For all of you who are solid believers, but need that something "extra" to help you believe for the supernatural to come into your life, I dedicate this book to you.

# Table of Contents

### Activating Your Personal Faith to Receive
*25 Biblical Principles for Releasing the Power Within!*

# Introduction

Jesus said in **Mark 9:23**, *"Everything is possible for him who be-lieves."* Believing is activating your personal faith. If you can get faith into your spirit then God will work in a miraculous way. But where does faith come from? How can we get it?

### Romans 10:17

*"So then faith comes by hearing, and hearing by the word of God." (NKJV)*

If you don't have faith, you can get faith to come to you and live in your heart. If you have family and friends who are in need and they don't have faith, read to them the Word of God. Faith comes by hearing the Word of God! You cannot see God work without faith; without faith it is impossible to please Him.

Faith is a choice, an act of the human will. It is a deliberate choice to place confidence in God and His Word. Unbelief is a sin because it is a deliberate choice to withhold confidence in God and His Word.

Faith is a receiving of the truth, an embracing of the truth, a commitment to the truth—and to the God of truth! And com-mitment always produces action. That is why faith without works is dead (James 2:17). With no action there is no commitment. With no commitment there is no faith!

In this book, you will find 25 faith-building principles that will enlarge your capacity to receive the very best that God has to offer you.

*Have Faith!*
*Rich Brott*

# The Principle of Bountiful Sowing

### 2 Corinthians 9:6

*"But this I say, He which soweth sparingly shall reap also sparingly; and he which soweth bountifully shall reap also bountifully." (KJV)*

I was raised in the farm country of Iowa. Both my father and I still own farmland, albeit a very small acreage when compared with full-time farmers. One thing we have learned is that you don't skimp in the areas of field preparation, the planting of seed, and the constant oversight of the crop. When we plant good seed, in good soil, we will reap a harvest. It's the law of the land, the law of God and one that must be followed. There always is the planting of the seed before the reaping of a harvest.

One certainly could not imagine that a farmer would expect to reap a great harvest by scattering a few seeds over an entire field. That would be like a Christian deciding not to tithe or give offerings, but rather just "tip" God with a few dollars here and there. Can you imagine a farmer, loaded with personal debt and residual bills saying to himself in early spring, "You know, I've got so many bills that need to be paid that I really can't afford to sow seed this year." You know without a doubt that any farmer in his right mind is going to put everything aside for now until he has sowed enough good seed in good ground to ensure a great personal harvest. The only way he is going to have a harvest is by scattering much seed so that it will multiply.

The only way to get anything out of his field is to put something into it. It is like giving our blood on a regular basis to a blood bank to be used for hospitals in need. When you sow in this area, what happens? You give your blood away and it multiplies. It reproduces itself. You can give it away again and again to persons in need. I was once the recipient of someone's blood. I needed it to sustain my life. Your blood replenishes itself so you can sow again and again.

As a young boy growing up, when we did not have enough food to put on the table, I watched my dad give all he had left in his bank account to various needs of the local church. Not just one time, but time and time again. And you know that it sounds very unreasonable—even illogical—to give when you are in desperate need yourself. That is why it takes faith to do so. God says that His ways are not like our ways. And that's a good thing! My dad learned that when you have a need, plant a seed!

If you skimp on the amount of the seed, the reaping will be sparse. If you plant a bountiful supply of seed, you will also reap bountifully. It is actually very simple. The more generous you are with the seed, the more generous the harvest. Seed reproduces itself. It multiplies!

# The Principle of
# Eternal Investments

### Matthew 6:19–21

*"Do not store up for yourselves treasures on earth, where moth and rust destroy, and where thieves break in and steal. But store up for yourselves treasures in heaven, where moth and rust do not destroy, and where thieves do not break in and steal. For where your treasure is, there your heart will be also."*

Most of us understand what we classify as earthly treasures. This list includes possessions such as cars, boats, clothes, houses, bank accounts, jewelry, portfolios, etc. But these things have no eternal value.

In Scripture, Jesus warns us about protecting our hearts from the love of these things, all of which can seem so real, so lasting, so concrete, but in reality can disappear so quickly. They can literally be here today and gone tomorrow.

Saul, an Old Testament king, was told to utterly destroy the Amalekites, his enemy. In Samuel 15, Scripture tells us that he decided to keep the spoils of war for himself. Because he disobeyed God, his kingdom was taken from him. He lost everything because he loved earthly treasures. This story is not so different than the New Testament story of the rich young ruler. He too had many things of earthly value. Are "things" wrong? Not necessarily. But they are a great distraction to the purpose of God. Earthly treasures can disrupt kingdom business. Are there "things" you are holding too close that could ultimately keep you from reaching your full potential in Christ? Or even worse, make you lose your soul because of their influence?

Death is the great equalizer, the constant leveler. Some of the ancient tombs discovered in the Middle East have been found packed with food and furniture, as well as slaves. Yet all of those buried remains, buried under sand for thousands of years, have done nothing for the one who spent a lifetime accumulating them.

Our stock portfolios are always at great risk to the ups and downs of the market, wars and rumors of wars, the economy of the nation and world, and the integrity of the company management in which we invest. Our bodies and our minds, which seem so healthy and sharp, may be wasted by disease or crushed by a mishap tomorrow.

We invest in what we care about. If we invest our money with God, we will be interested in the ministry advance of our local church and will pray for the expansion of His kingdom locally and globally.

Note in the Matthew 6 passage that Jesus is not saying to have nothing, enjoy nothing, or that possessions are a sin. Christ is telling us to not get too tied to these things. Be a conduit, not a dam. It is not about what we have, but what has us. If you center your life on things, if you base your living upon possessions, you will for sure be disappointed.

Don't base your life, your future, your well-being, or your happiness on the things you have accumulated. Instead, be sure you lay up for yourself the real treasures, the ones that will be of eternal value.

Notice the tone of this Scripture (Matthew 6:19–21). It doesn't seem to be a suggestion, rather a definite command of sorts. It is no secret that the rich attract a lot of interested people. While he has money, everyone wants to be near him. Should his riches disappear, so will his friends. Not much different from a beautiful, talented young actress, singer, or musician. When her beauty fades or talent diminishes, the world looks for another to admire.

In days gone by, people accumulated wealth by the garments they possessed, the fields of grain that fed their families, and the gold that was used to barter for other things they needed or desired. When Jesus warned of storing earthly treasures, He knew what He was talking about. When it comes to moths, expensive clothes can be destroyed very easily. Grain can be lost to fungus and insects. Thieves can quickly make your gold disappear.

Many of the homes constructed in the ancient Middle East were made with sun-baked clay or loose stones. Although adequate for housing, it presented a comparatively easy way for thieves to dig under or through the wall or enter by other means. No possessions were safe from those that would steal.

Of course, we know that rust can destroy even the best of tools, and moths also attack things we consume. Literally, rust in its destructive path will eat into and destroy nearly everything. Rust will eventually corrode all metal, including silver and gold. Figuratively speaking, rust can be anything that destroys you and your life. In short, all your treasures, whether physical or otherwise, can be destroyed.

The possessions we accumulate in this world are temporary at best. Each of the three metaphors found in Matthew 6:19–21 tell us together that life is short and futile. Any of these things, when expanded to include those things from today's culture that can destroy, clearly demonstrate to us the folly of putting our trust in earthly possessions. Bad investments or good investments pilfered away by bad management or dishonest CEOs can make our lifetime of savings disappear overnight.

It's not that saving or storing assets is sinful in itself. Paul notes in 2 Corinthians 12:14 that parents ought to save up for their children. When increase comes our way, we should use it, not only for our needs, but also for the good of others.

Treasures on earth can become paths to building heavenly treasures if they are used and distributed for the glory of God. Jesus understood clearly that in the consumer culture of this world, a constant battle for our affections, our hearts, and our souls rages.

- "Our callings are not simply secular means of making money or a living, but are God's means of utilizing our gifts and interests to His glory." —a paraphrase of Martin Luther (1483–1546)

- "Alas, how many, even among those who are called believers, have plenty of all the necessities of life, and yet complain of poverty!" —John Wesley (1703–1791)

- "Money never made a man happy yet, nor will it. There is nothing in its nature to produce happiness. The more a man has, the more he wants. Instead of filling a vacuum, it makes one. If it satisfies one want, it doubles and triples that want another way. That was a true proverb of the wise man, rely upon it; 'Better is little with the fear of the Lord, than great treasure, and trouble therewith.'" —Benjamin Franklin (1706–1790)

# The Principle of Giving Cheerfully

### 2 Corinthians 9:7

*"Every man according as he purposeth in his heart, so let him give; not grudgingly, or of necessity: for God loveth a cheerful giver." (KJV)*

What kind of giver are you? Are you a person who gives grudgingly, or are you the kind of person God loves—a cheerful giver? A cheerful giver receives great happiness, so much that the giver's own challenges and personal pain is soon forgotten. Following is the story of one such giver.

This story is about a beautiful, expensively dressed lady who complained to her psychiatrist that she felt that her whole life was empty; it had no meaning. The counselor called over the old lady who cleaned the office floors and said to the rich lady, "I'm going to ask Mary here to tell you how she found happiness. All I want you to do is listen."

So the old lady put down her broom and sat on a chair and told her story:

> *"Well, my husband died of malaria, and three months later my only son was killed by a car. I had nobody... I had nothing left. I couldn't sleep; I couldn't eat; I never smiled at anyone; I even thought of taking my own life. Then one evening a little kitten followed me home from work. Somehow I felt sorry for that kitten. It was cold outside, so I decided to let the kitten in. I got it some milk, and it licked the plate clean. Then it purred and rubbed against my leg, and for the first time in months I smiled.*

*Then I stopped to think. If helping a little kitten could make me smile, maybe doing something for people could make me happy. So the next day I baked some biscuits and took them to a neighbor who was sick in bed. Every day I tried to do some-thing nice for someone. It made me so happy to see them happy. Today I don't know of anybody who sleeps and eats better than I do. I've found happiness by giving it to others."*

When she heard that, the rich lady cried. She had everything money could buy, but she had lost the things which money cannot buy. (Source Unknown)

# *The Principle of*
# *Leaving It All Behind*

### *I Timothy 6:7*

*"For we brought nothing into the world, and we can take nothing out of it."*

It's pretty tough to read this Scripture and come away with any other thought. It is simple yet profound. Short yet meaningful. We all should remind ourselves of this every day. The following is a very meaningful story that was written by Dr. Billy Graham.

A little child was playing one day with a very valuable vase. He put his hand into it and could not withdraw it. His father too tried his best, but all in vain. They were thinking of breaking the vase when the father said, "Now, my son, make one more try. Open your hand and hold your fingers out straight as you see me doing, and then pull." To their astonishment the little fellow said, "Oh no, father. I couldn't put my fingers out like that, because if I did I would drop my penny." Smile, if you will—but thousands of us are like that little boy, so busy holding on to the world's worthless penny that we cannot accept liberation. I beg you to drop the trifle in your heart. Surrender! Let go!

# The Principle of Misplaced Trust

**Proverbs 11:28**

*"Whoever trusts in his riches will fall, but the righteous will thrive like a green leaf." (NASB)*

Many people live life just for themselves. Many seek self-fulfillment, oblivious to the plight of the world around them. Some seek to become wealthy, not to bless others, but to serve themselves up with the good life. The last words a person articulates just before dying come directly from the heart. Napoleon Bonaparte, the legendary French general, is reported to have said as he lay dying, "I am dying before my time and my body is going to return to the earth. This is the fate of the man we called Napoleon the Great."

Voltaire, author and philosopher (1694–1778), was born Francois-Marie Arouet November 21, 1694, in Paris. Voltaire's intelligence, wit, and style made him one of France's greatest writers and philosophers. He received his education at a Jesuit College in Paris.

While his humorous verses made him a favorite in society circles, in 1717 his sharp wit got him into trouble with the authorities. He was imprisoned in the Bastille for eleven months for writing a scathing satire of the French government. Voltaire spent much of his life endeavoring to undermine Christianity. He attempted to undercut a Christian believer's faith and his or her hopes in the eternal life of the hereafter. Yet when he came face-to-face with his own eternal destiny, he was afraid of what was coming next. On his deathbed, Voltaire is said to have confided these words to his doctor: "I have been abandoned by God and by men! I'll give you half my fortune if you extend my life by six months."

Be careful where you place your trust.

# The Principle of Momentary Possessions

### I Timothy 6:7–8

*"For we brought nothing into the world, and we can take nothing out of it."*

We do well to remember the fact that money and possessions are only temporary. At best, money only lasts a lifetime. At worst, it doesn't last at all. It is very fleeting, only a vapor, just like our lives. Why spend all of your life trying to accumulate something that will never last? How much better it would be for you to spend your time investing in things that are eternal in nature.

### Psalm 39:4

*"Show me, O Lord, my life's end and the number of my days; let me know how fleeting is my life."*

Don't spend all your life trying to accumulate something that will never last. How much better it would be to spend your time investing in things of an eternal nature. Being the recipient of God's provision and blessing and enjoying great wealth and prosperity is not meant for the purpose of accumulating temporary earthly gain. It is to be used to build a foundation for heavenly gain. Instead of hoarding it all for personal enjoyment, it is to be used to further the kingdom of God. Any prosperity you gain on this earth is because you have learned good stewardship principles. The biblical prosperity here in this life is but a foreshadowing of things to come on the other side.

At the end of your life, will you look back and wish you had owned a bigger home or a nicer car or that you had spent more time with your family and friends? The only thing you can (and will) take out of this life is your soul. How much time do you spend daily pursuing eternal possessions instead of temporal ones?

On Judgment Day, will God be able to say to you, "Well done, My good and faithful servant"? Will He be pleased with the way you spent your days here on earth, or will He be saddened by the amount of time you wasted on accumulating material possessions instead of eternal ones?

Possessions are temporary! Don't make the mistake of holding on to them too tightly. Job understood this when he said in 1:20, "Naked I came from my mother's womb, and naked I will depart. The Lord gave and the Lord has taken away; may the name of the Lord be praised."

It may be pleasant to accumulate many comforts of living, but just be sure you understand their temporary value and nature. To spend a lifetime gathering temporary possessions but neglecting the important treasures that last an eternity would be very foolish indeed. Don't get so focused on the here and now that you fail to think and see eternally. Treasure those things that have eternal and kingdom value because the only treasure worth possessing is kingdom treasure.

### Matthew 6:19–21

*"Do not store up for yourselves treasures on earth, where moth and rust destroy, and where thieves break in and steal. But store up for yourselves treasures in heaven, where moth and rust do not destroy, and where thieves do not break in and steal. For where your treasure is, there your heart will be also."*

### Psalm 89:47

*"Remember how fleeting is my life. For what futility you have created all men!"*

### Proverbs 21:6

*"A fortune made by a lying tongue is a fleeting vapor and a deadly snare."*

# The Principle of
# Money According to Jesus

Jesus had some things to say about money and its affect upon our lives.

- We are definitely rewarded for the deeds done in the body. In other words, we are only rewarded for those deeds accomplished while we are alive. While we are alive, true life does not consist in the abundance of material things (Luke 12:15).

- Prosperity is much more than acquiring personal monetary wealth! Be sure that money doesn't have you, instead of you having it (Luke 18:18–23; Matthew 19:21–22; Mark 12:41–44).

- Give according to your income, unless you prefer that God makes your income proportionate to your giving! There is such a thing as becoming "rich" toward God, as one refrains from being preoccupied with materialistic concerns (Luke 12:21).

- Giving God what is His is a parallel duty to one's faithful payment of his taxes (Matthew 22:21; Mark 12:13–17; Malachi 3:8).

- We should not make a public "show" of giving. By doing so, we may have already received the only recognition we deserve (Matthew 6:1–4).

- Life priorities are very important to understand. What is the most important thing for you to acquire? Is it the love of your family? How about serving your loved ones, your church, and your neighbor? How about ones, your church, and your neighbor? How about your good health and honorable character? You can't serve God if you are fascinated only by money (Matthew 6:24–34; 19:21–22).

- God uses willing people in imaginative ways. In God's eyes giving even a cup of water can bring a reward (Matthew 10:41).

- Everything we have belongs to God. We are allowed to be temporary stewards of His wealth. Embracing "kingdom treasures" requires a "releasing" attitude toward earthly resources (Matthew 13:44–46).

- You are laying up treasure either in heaven or on earth. Everything you have you will ultimately lose. Gaining earthly abundance is an unworthy goal if you forfeit spiritual priorities (Matthew 16:26).

- The Dead Sea takes in and takes in, but it never gives anything out; hence it is stagnant. Stinginess is a characteristic of those who don't understand the extent of their forgiveness. The Sea of Galilee takes in, but it also gives out; for this reason it is filled with life, and its water is fresh. (Matthew 18:27; Luke 19:8–9).

- Putting the needs of others first will be rewarded. Sacrifice of self-interest for the kingdom will be compensated a hundredfold (Matthew 19:29–30; Luke 18:28–30).

- Talent is on loan from God. We did not deserve God's love and forgiveness. Possessions and talent are a responsibility entrusted to us. We are responsible to multiply those gifts and funds entrusted to us (Matthew 25:14–30; Luke 19:11–27).

- God so loved the world that He gave His only Son. He gave His best. Are you giving your best? Are you sharing what you have with others? What you give will be bountifully multiplied back to you (Luke 6:38).

- What we are is far more important than what we possess. A wise "handling" of people and money illustrates a spiritual sensitivity to God's kingdom "rules" of finance (Luke 16:1–13).

- God never promised a reward for those who give away their money after they are dead and gone. To will your material goods to charity doesn't help you in your relationship to God. Wealth is not prohibited, but this admonition points to the compassionless lifestyle it can breed (Luke 18:24–27; 16:19–31).

- The size of the gift is not so important, rather, the ability of the giver. Our giving is made "great" in the proportion it represents and by the cheerful and generous spirit that prompts it (Mark 12:41–44; Luke 21:1–4).

# The Principle of
# Money Stewardship

### Luke 16:11–12

*"So if you have not been trustworthy in handling worldly wealth, who will trust you with true riches? And if you have not been trustworthy with someone else's property, who will give you property of your own?"*

Every human being alive must be a steward of personal resources of skill, knowledge, strength, possessions, and influence. We don't need to necessarily aspire for more or feel discouraged about areas of what we may perceive as lack; we just need to use what we have. Hard work, efficient use of our available resources, and a disciplined personal life will lead to prosperity and success. Os Guinness said, "Ownership is God's; stewardship is ours."

### Matthew 25:24–28

*"Then the man with the $1,000 came and said, 'Sir, I knew you were a hard man, and I was afraid you would rob me of what I earned, so I hid your money in the earth and here it is!' But his master replied, 'Wicked man! Lazy slave! Since you knew I would demand your profit, you should at least have put my money into the bank so I could have some interest. Take the money from this man and give it to the man with the $10,000.'" (RSV)*

In Matthew 25:14–30, the parable of the talents is recorded. This story tells of a certain man who distributed his wealth among three servants, giving to each according to his ability. As this parable would imply, our abilities vary individually, and it is wise for us to realize that this is true also in our ability to earn money.

The parable proceeds to tell how each man invested his seed money. The first two traded theirs—that is, they used it—and in the process they doubled the amount they had originally. The last person, however, tried to hoard or keep his by doing nothing with it. In the end, each had to account for his actions.

The man with only two talents, through his small ability and industry, gained a 100 percent increase, and he was promoted. He was responsible only to use the ability he had to do the best he could do. What about the man who had one talent? According to the Bible, his complaining and whining attitude was not well received. His employer, though critical, was just in his actions. He told the slothful servant that he could have tried at the least to obtain help from others by placing the talent into the hands of those who knew what to do with it.

Instead, the man chose idleness. He was cast away and punished, not because he misused the talent or lost it or sold it, but because he did nothing with it. God expects us to be doing what we are able to do with what He has committed to us. If we apply ourselves and use the talents He has given us, He will bless us. If you are a good steward over a little, then God looks at you and thinks, I can trust this person with more.

### Revelation 2:23

*"I will repay each of you according to your deeds."*

# The Principle of No Greed

### Luke 12:16–19

*"The ground of a certain rich man produced a good crop. He thought to himself, 'What shall I do? I have no place to store my crops.' Then he said, 'This is what I'll do. I will tear down my barns and build bigger ones, and there I will store all my grain and my goods."*

We live in an age of self-indulgence. Is it different than any previous age or just the same self-serving pleasure in a different culture? This Scripture covers the subject well, so it is probably the latter. Here we have the story of a prominent businessperson who was not satisfied with what he had. Is this bad? Not necessarily. It is proper for a businessperson to grow the business and expand the facilities and capacity of the company. It may mean new factory space to make room for new manufactured products. Maybe it is new warehouse space to house additional inventory. It might mean an expansion of current office space to be able to process new customers and a sales/service force. All of this is quite normal for a forward-thinking successful enterprise. God honors forward-thinking, preplanning, productivity, and personal diligence.

So what about this certain rich man? What was his problem? Everything appears normal at first glance. But something deep inside was not apparent perhaps to business associates, friends, and neighbors. While appearing very successful on the outside, the inside rang hallow. Apparently he had planned for the present, but gave no thought to planning for his future. He had not prepared for his afterlife. All of the temporary preplanning was going on, but the most important decision in his life, that of the life to come, had not been made. The clarification came as Jesus said that one who stores up material wealth without storing up spiritual riches as well is just plain misdirected, misguided, and foolish.

First Timothy 6:10 says this: "For the love of money is a root of all kinds of evil. Some people, eager for money, have wandered from the faith and pierced themselves with many griefs."

It's okay to build your friendships, have a career, become successful, grow a business, prepare for retirement, accumulate wealth, and so on. But in the process of looking out for yourself, don't neglect the spiritual man. Don't forget why God desires to bless you. Prepare yourself to be a blessing to others…in this life.

Ecclesiastes 5:10–17 speaks to human nature and how careful we must be not to be one who is consumed with the love of money.

He who loves money shall never have enough. The foolishness of thinking that wealth brings happiness! The more you have, the more you spend, right up to the limits of your income. So what is the advantage of wealth—except perhaps to watch it as it runs through your fingers! The man who works hard sleeps well whether he eats little or much, but the rich must worry and suffer insomnia.

There is another serious problem I have seen everywhere—savings are put into risky investments that turn sour, and soon there is nothing left to pass on to one's son. The man who speculates is soon back to where he began-with nothing. This, as I said, is a very serious problem, for all his hard work has been for nothing; he has been working for the wind. It is all swept away. All the rest of his life he is under a cloud-gloomy, discouraged, frustrated, and angry. (TLB)

# The Principle of
# Not Withholding

### Proverbs 11:24–28

*"One man gives freely, yet gains even more; another withholds unduly, but comes to poverty."*

We gain by giving. We lose by withholding! You may recall the story about the widow and her son who were about to eat their last meal, as noted in 1 Kings 17. After that, they assumed they would just starve to death because they had no more food available, and there was a famine in the land. In our culture today, this is very hard for many of us to comprehend.

Some people teach that we should give to get. Others teach that we should sacrifice and withhold from our family in order to give more. Neither extreme point of view is correct. We must provide for our family. We should not give to get. Our attitude should be one of obedience and liberality. The best way to give to the Lord is to understand all that He has given to us, and then freely give back to Him.

God removes His blessings from those who withhold. He cannot bless an act of disobedience. Our money becomes a curse when we think more of it than we do of God. One of the greatest privileges God has allowed us is to participate in the blessing of regular tithing and the giving of offerings.

When we freely give to God, regardless of our own personal need, we allow God to be big in our lives. We allow Him to provide for us. This can only happen as we buy into the principle of freely giving. If we are stingy in our giving and withhold from the Lord, we miss the many blessings and provisions He wants to shower upon us.

# The Principle of Obedience in Giving

### Malachi 3:10

*"Bring the whole tithe into the storehouse, that there may be food in my house."*

The Scripture here is very clear in its message. It does not begin with a thought or suggestion about something to consider. It simply begins with the word bring. The word bring means to carry, fetch, or transport. What are we instructed to bring? Not only the tithe, but we are told to bring the "whole tithe." Where are we to bring it? We are to bring it into the storehouse—our local church. That means the place of our worship, the storehouse that feeds us. We are not to send part of our tithe to some distant place, but rather we are to bring the whole tithe into the house that feeds us. The reason is so simple yet profound—so that there can be finances for operation and evangelism (food in the storehouse). God always blesses our obedience. He wants to bless us in the best possible way, but that can only happen as a result of our obedience.

# The Principle of
# Personal Finance

There are four important principles with regard to personal finance.

## 1. God Owns Everything!

When you understand this first principle, you will be in a right position to prosper; you will then be able to make God your partner. Prospering by partnering with God is first done by accepting this fact. God owns everything! You do not own anything. You may have a business that you operate or manage, but you are only doing what God has allowed you to do. Christians don't own anything at all; they merely manage things for God. When you die, how much of your money will you leave behind? All of it! When you die, how much of your money will you take with you? None of it!

Ultimately, you don't own anything. You won't take your house with you. You won't take your land with you. You won't take any of the wealth or possessions with you that you have managed to accumulate here on earth. You won't even take your body because you don't even own it. When your spirit leaves your body, it will turn to dust. You may currently possess certain things, but mere possession is not ownership. Those things that you possess can be taken from you in an instant.

**Psalm 24:1**

*"The earth is the Lord's, and everything in it, the world, and all who live in it."*

**Haggai 2:8**

*"'The silver is mine and the gold is mine,' declares the Lord Almighty."*

### Psalm 50:10–11

*"For every animal of the forest is mine, and the cattle on a thousand hills. I know every bird in the mountains, and the creatures of the field are mine."*

You can possess, but it is God who owns. You may earn a living, but it is God who gives you the ability to earn.

## 2. How Money Is Obtained

The principles upon which a person builds his financial future are very important. They can ensure security in the later years of a person's life. The manner in which finances are acquired and disbursed must be based on sound moral guidelines. Desire for money can become an obsession. When it does, nothing can satisfy. Peace of mind is gone. The joy of a new day gives way to worry about retaining what one has and gaining more and more.

If God cannot trust you with a hundred dollars now, how can He trust you with a thousand or a hundred thousand? Christians have access to unlimited and unimaginable resources. But with this access comes accountability. If you don't take care of that old clunker of a vehicle you now own, how can you care for a new car? If you goof off during the day at your current job, why would God want to bless you with a better one? If you cannot take good care of the apartment or house you rent, how can you be trusted with your own property? There is a principle at work here! We must prove that we can be good stewards.

Our life's stewardship should reflect God's interest in all that He has entrusted us with. Genesis 1:26 records that God made man to rule over all the earth and all life on earth, both plant and animal. In Genesis 2:15, man was made steward over the Garden, in which there was gold, precious stones, and rivers. In other words, man was created for more than going to heaven after a lifetime of waiting. He was created to be a faithful steward over the work of God's hands.

This is a lot of trust that God places in our lives. It is more than just finances. It is our entire life and how we handle it with faithfulness, responsibility, accountability, honesty, and integrity. Stewardship is bringing everything we have to offer under the lordship of Christ. What kind of a person makes a good steward? A person who has a great respect for God and His creation.

The Bible also indicates that one's control of the finances in his possession is a direct indication of the control he exercises in spiritual matters. If a person cannot handle God's blessing of finance, it is likely that he cannot handle too much time on his hands, promotion on the job, authority on the job, authority in the church, and probably a whole host of other spiritual issues. The "unjust steward" of Luke 16 had other personal problems besides just being a bad manager for his lord. His dishonesty became very apparent when he was about to lose his job. The handling of a person's financial affairs is closely akin to his or her other values. The value system of one's heart is exposed by his relationship to money and material things. The rich young ruler is another illustration of that fact (see Matthew 19:16–22).

Money and possessions, at best, only last a lifetime. At worst, they don't last at all. They are but a fleeting vapor, just like our lives. Why spend all of your life trying to accumulate something that will never last? How much better it would be for you to spend your time investing in things that are of eternal value.

Some of the most miserable people in the world are people who literally "have everything." Everything, that is, except a loving family and a clean heart! Everything except honor. Everything except the blessing of God. The Lord has better things to come for those who have been good stewards of all He has entrusted to them.

Leaving all scruples and morals for the sake of money is a foolish thing to do. Yet that is just what many men and women are doing today. And their seemingly apparent success sometimes causes an infectious greed that hangs upon people who should know better. Some people don't strive to put in an honest day's work for an honest dollar—a day's work for a day's pay. They get caught up in the spirit of the "fast buck." Easy money...unearned income...get rich quick!

God is concerned about our actions and motives. The person who takes stewardship seriously handles life, talents, strength, and money as a trust from God.

### 3. How Money Is Disbursed

There is nothing wrong or evil about money itself. It is just a medium of exchange for goods or services rendered. However, there is often something wrong with our attitude toward money. We always seem to want more than we have. This dissatisfaction with our current state or condition can be blamed on our Adamic human nature. Discontentment and coveting what belongs to another can cause problems with money. Paul wrote in I Timothy 6:9, "But they that will be rich fall into temptation and a snare, and into many foolish and hurtful lusts."

Many people who have lived for money and success have failed God. When a person's attitude is not right toward money, he or she may fall into the trap of materialism. If, on the other hand, we use the monetary blessings God has given us to finance His cause and further His kingdom, we will be blessed accordingly. *I Timothy 6:7* reminds us, *"For we brought nothing into this world, and it is certain we can carry nothing out."*

- *"For in him we live and move and have our being" (**Deuteronomy 8:18**).*

- *"But remember the Lord your God, for it is He who gives you the ability to produce wealth" (**Acts 17:28**).*

- *"For every living soul belongs to me" (**Ezekiel 18:4**).*

- *"Therefore, I urge you, brothers, in view of God's mercy, to offer your bodies as living sacrifices, holy and pleasing to God" (**Romans 12:1**).*

- *"Know that the Lord is God. It is he who made us, and we are his; we are his people, the sheep of his pasture"* (**Psalm 100:3**).

- *"You are not your own; you were bought at a price. Therefore honor God with your body"* (**1 Corinthians 6:19–20**).

Because we are not our own, we should dedicate to God all that we are, all that we own, and all that we will ever be. You are God's, so all you have belongs to Him. You simply manage your possessions for Him. Your business belongs to God. When everything you have belongs to God, it takes all of the pressure off you. For example, let's say you are a farmer and your farm belongs to God. If the weather is dry and it doesn't rain, you don't have to worry about it because it belongs to God. If your business is dedicated to God, it becomes His problem and not yours. In business, when you partner with God, He not only will bless it, but He will also let you enjoy prosperity. But there is a caution not to keep everything to yourself. Instead of trying to figure out how little to give God, try giving it all to Him and ask Him how much you should keep.

### 4. How Money Is Contributed

There is certainly nothing wrong with making money, so long as making money does not violate the laws of our land and the principles of God's Word. The all-for-me and none-for-others way of man's thinking is immoral. The person of principle who subscribes to the values of the Bible will be a good steward who obeys the law of giving. This person will find happiness in exact proportion to the degree that he gives. He will be content with his life and all that it affords.

The apostle Paul realized that although everything in the universe belongs to God, if we partner with Him, He allows us to keep some of everything He provides. The farmer who harvests the crop has a right to eat some of it. The one who plants the vineyard gets to enjoy some of its fruit.

In business, when you partner with God, He not only will bless it; He will also let you enjoy prosperity. When we become Christians, we become children of God. And the Bible says that God wants to give gifts to His children.

But God also wants to be sure that we are more interested in pleasing Him than pleasing ourselves. What is your motive for being in business? Is it to accumulate money and possessions so that you can hoard it all for yourself? Or are you in business to help and bless others? God is interested in your motives. Can you be trusted with prosperity? Jesus said in Matthew 6:33, "Seek ye first the kingdom of God, and his righteousness; and all these things shall be added unto you." Our motives and priorities must be: God first, me last.

A musician and prophet in Old Testament times by the name of Asaph said, *"I was envious at the foolish, when I saw the prosperity of the wicked"* (**Psalm 73:3**).

There are ungodly men and women who may achieve material prosperity apart from God. But they can never achieve the deep settled peace that comes from God. Riches gained without God are a snare and do not bring peace. But prosperity that comes from God brings not only an abundance of possessions, but also emotional peace, happiness, and great joy. Do you know why some very wicked people are rich today? The Bible gives us a very simple explanation. The wicked who are rich are simply holding the wealth that someday God will give to His children.

- *"And the wealth of the sinner is laid up for the righteous"* (**Proverbs 13:22, ASV**).

- *"Give, and it shall be given unto you"* (**Luke 6:38**).

When you give to the kingdom of God, it will be given back to you. But where will it come from? Who will give to you? Will God cause money to float down from the heavenlies so that your needs will be met? No. The rest of that verse says, "shall men give into your...[life]." When you give to God, God in turn causes others to give to you. This could be in the form of new customers to your business, new products to sell, and so on.

When God owns your business, He will make sure it prospers! Giving is the trigger for God's financial miracles. Nothing happens in the economy of God until you give something away. It is a universal law of God. Paul said *"Remember this:Whoever sows sparingly will also reap sparingly, and whoever sows generously will also reap generously"* (**2 Corinthians 9:6**).

# The Principle of
# Personal Giftings

Each of us has been given access to gifts from God. Are you developing that gift? Are you using and exercising the gifting of God? If God has blessed you with houses and lands, businesses and possessions, are you trusting only in them and pursuing more of the same, or are you developing good stewardship over them? If these things mean a lot to you and you give all your time and all your money to seeking more, than be careful, because you won't have them forever. However, if you are pursuing God and the things of His kingdom, He will probably trust you with more.

If we are idle and lazy, we will be judged accordingly (Ecclesiastes 10:18). At judgment day we will give an account for every idle word we speak (Matthew 12:36). If we must account for an idle word, what about idle time? The apostle Paul encouraged the Ephesians to redeem the time (5:16). The Greek word is exagorazo and means "to buy up" or "rescue from loss" (Strong's Concordance).

A great lesson can be learned from the Matthew 25:14–25 parable of the talents. When God invests something in our lives and allows us to have stewardship over it, we must use it for His glory and His kingdom. If we do nothing with it, God will take it away and give it to another. If we do not know how to invest it into the kingdom or how to take care of it, we had better seek some wisdom. God is very interested in our caretaking ability and what we do with our time, money, possessions, and ministry giftings. What we do, where we go, and the actions we take are very important to God. Remember, we are not the owners of all God has given us, we are only stewards—we are managers and therefore responsible and accountable for the gifts and for their use.

In addition to the stewardship of our giftings, consider the gifting of our stewardship. The biblical story of the poor widow models how our gifting stewardship should be.

### Luke 21:1–3

*"As he looked up, Jesus saw the rich putting their gifts into the temple treasury. He also saw a poor widow put in two very small copper coins. 'I tell you the truth,' he said, 'this poor widow has put in more than all the others. All these people gave their gifts out of their wealth; but she out of her poverty put in all she had to live on.'"*

The widow was poor, perhaps destitute. She had a couple of coins to pay for her next meal or two, but that's it. Her desire to give to God was so powerful that she pulled both coins from her pocket and gave all she had.

She gave cheerfully to the work of the kingdom. No one saw her do it. No one knew what she gave. No one understood that she gave it all. No one even noticed—no one, except Jesus. Jesus knew the depth of her sacrifice. Jesus knew what it cost her. All of the other givers on that day gave out of their abundance, out of their wealth. She gave out of her poverty.

This woman is a model for us to have the right motivation in giving. When Jesus spoke about giving in His Sermon on the Mount, He taught that the motivation for giving should not be to receive the praise of men or to impress people with our wealth or generosity. Instead, we should be so focused on pleasing God (more than men) that we do not even allow others to see that we are giving.

### Matthew 6:1–4

*"Take heed that you do not do your charitable deeds before men, to be seen by them. Otherwise you have no reward from your Father in heaven. Therefore, when you do a charitable deed, do not sound a trumpet before you as the hypocrites do in the synagogues and in the streets, that*

*they may have glory from men. Assuredly, I say to you, they have their reward. But when you do a charitable deed, do not let your left hand know what your right hand is doing, that your charitable deed may be in secret; and your Father who sees in secret will himself reward you openly."* (NKJV)

# The Principle of
# Personal Accountability

Christians have access to unlimited and unimaginable resources. Along with this access comes accountability. One of the greatest motivators, and probably the biggest single need regarding stewardship, is accountability.

Accountability begins with the person, not the gifts. Accountability in the human sense is recognized favorably by any society and rewarded accordingly. A profound illustration of this principle taken from biblical times is found in the life of Joseph. It seems that in every job he had, he started at the bottom and eventually landed at the top (see Genesis 39–41).

Joseph was tested severely on many occasions: he was lied about, cheated on, and forgotten for two years by a man for whom he had done a great favor. What was his secret of success? Joseph was a hard worker, and no matter what job he was assigned, he went after it with efficiency, enthusiasm, and energy! And to his credit, Joseph never allowed temporary adversity to make him bitter. He always had a great positive attitude, and he maintained a devout trust in God. God honors effort and will always bless those who are giving their best.

Accountability is the responsibility of people in all economic situations. It doesn't matter how rich, how poor, how educated, or how illiterate. The Old Testament includes a story of a very poor woman's accountability. A woman who had very little by way of possessions, yet obedience and accountability was required of her.

### I Kings 17:8–16

*"Then the word of the Lord came to him: 'Go at once to Zarephath of Sidon and stay there. I have commanded a widow in that place to supply you with food.' So he went to Zarephath. When he came to the town gate, a widow was there gathering sticks. He called to her and asked, 'Would you bring me a little water in a jar so I may have a drink?' As she was going to get it, he called, 'And bring me, please, a piece of bread.' 'As surely as the Lord your God lives,' she replied, 'I don't have any bread—only a handful of flour in a jar and a little oil in a jug. I am gathering a few sticks to take home and make a meal for myself and my son, that we may eat it—and die.' Elijah said to her, 'Don't be afraid. Go home and do as you have said. But first make a small cake of bread for me from what you have and bring it to me, and then make something for yourself and your son. For this is what the Lord, the God of Israel, says: 'The jar of flour will not be used up and the jug of oil will not run dry until the day the Lord gives rain on the land.'' She went away and did as Elijah had told her. So there was food every day for Elijah and for the woman and her family. For the jar of flour was not used up and the jug of oil did not run dry, in keeping with the word of the Lord spoken by Elijah."*

This story is about a woman who was accountable to God in faith and obedience to meet the need of another with what she had in her household. Elijah was dependent on God's provision through this poor widow, one who had almost nothing and was ready to die. This woman was in a famine, a time to be very careful and self-protecting, but the famine was not in her spirit. She had a generous and giving spirit. The famine could not break her; her generosity could not be bound. She gave from her need and poverty, from what she had in her household.

This story shows that even if you think you are lacking, God can use the things you do have to meet a need. You may think you just don't have the money to give right now, or you may think that because you have very little, God will excuse you from your responsibility to be fully accountable with what you do have. Not so. God expects accountability from people of all socioeconomic classes.

If you cannot afford to give largely, you must not despise the day of small beginnings. God never asks us to give what we do not have. He only asks that we be willing to give all we do have. Second Corinthians 8:12 shows us that it is the heart that matters: "For if the willingness is there, the gift is acceptable according to what one has, not according to what he does not have." We can look to the needs and then look to our own household, listening to and obeying the voice of the Holy Spirit when He says, "Give."

Like this widow, we too will experience seasons of testing. Enduring such seasons will teach us faith and trust in God. We must not allow a spirit of poverty to bind us, choke us, or keep us from giving. If you are experiencing a season like this right now, I encourage you to take the words of Elijah to heart. In 1 Kings 17:3, he tells the widow, "Do not be afraid." When in doubt, we must believe the words of hope that fill the Scriptures, not fearing what our minds or circumstances may say to us. As we put fear aside, we move into the realm of faith, trusting God to provide for us, just as He did for the widow of Zarephath.

# The Principle of
# Seeking Financial Wisdom

Scripture is very clear about matters of stewardship. It is also clear that when we struggle in areas of finance, we are to seek help from those who have knowledge and experience. Not understanding how to handle your finances correctly does not excuse you from the responsibility of good stewardship. Proverbs 17:16 says, "Of what use is money in the hand of a fool, since he has no desire to get wisdom?"

### Proverbs 24:3–6

*"Any enterprise is built by wise planning, becomes strong through common sense, and profits wonderfully by keeping abreast of the facts." (RSV)*

### Proverbs 15:22

*"Plans fail for lack of counsel, but with many advisers they succeed."*

Seeking wisdom and getting help is a personal responsibility, a biblical principle and a practical solution to any personal financial problems. It is your responsibility to get spiritual advice and wisdom about your financial decisions.

### Proverbs 4:5–7

*Get wisdom, get understanding; do not forget my words or swerve from them. Do not forsake wisdom, and she will protect you; love her, and she will watch over you. Wisdom is supreme; therefore get wisdom. Though it cost all you have, get understanding."*

You can have the best intentions regarding a bright financial future, but without input from others, your intentions will fail.

What people do you know in your own life (a church friend, coworker, pastor, CPA) who obviously have their finances in order? Approach them and ask for their advice. People love to share their ideas and strategies with others.

### Matthew 7:7–8

*"Ask and it will be given to you; seek and you will find; knock and the door will be opened to you. For everyone who asks receives; he who seeks finds; and to him who knocks, the door will be opened."*

Humble yourself and learn from those around you.

# The Principle of
## Knowing that Faith is a Choice

My giving is an indicator of whether or not I trust God and just how much I trust my life to Him. The following Scripture tells of rewards that come to those who seek Him. If I do not believe this and other similar passages in the Bible, I will not give generously, as I will feel the need to hold on tightly to what I have already accumulated in this life. My level of giving is an indication of where my heart is.

**Hebrews 11:6**

*"And without faith it is impossible to please God, because anyone who comes to him must believe that he exists and that he rewards those who earnestly seek him."*

**James 2:14–26**

*"What good is it, my brothers, if a man claims to have faith but has no deeds? Can such faith save him? In the same way, faith by itself, if it is not accompanied by action, is dead. But someone will say, "You have faith; I have deeds." Show me your faith without deeds, and I will show you my faith by what I do. You foolish man, do you want evidence that faith without deeds is useless? You see that his faith and his actions were working together, and his faith was made complete by what he did. You see that a person is justified by what he does and not by faith alone. As the body without the spirit is dead, so faith without deeds is dead."*

**John 1:1**

*"In the beginning was the Word and the Word was with God and the Word was God."*

God spoke the words of the Bible, God is behind every word, and God watches over every promise to make it good.

Jesus said in Mark 9:23, "Everything is possible for him who believes." Believing is activating your personal faith. If you can get faith into your spirit then God will work in a miraculous way. But where does faith come from? How can we get it?

**Romans 10:17**

*"So then faith comes by hearing, and hearing by the word of God." (NKJV)*

If you don't have faith, you can get faith to come to you and live in your heart. If you have family and friends who are in need and they don't have faith, read to them the Word of God. Faith comes by hearing the Word of God! You cannot see God work without faith; without faith it is impossible to please Him. The secret is to take in and give out the Word of God. There can be no salvation, no healing, no miracles, no answers to prayer...apart from Bible faith. And Bible faith only comes by hearing, receiving, and acting upon the promises in the Word of God. We prepare for answers to our prayers by receiving the faith that comes from God. Our preparation is the evidence of our faith.

Faith is not basically a feeling, although it produces feeling (Romans 15:13). Being a virtue and something we are commanded to do, faith becomes a choice.

**Mark 11:22**

*"Have faith in God."*

Faith is a choice, an act of the human will. It is a deliberate choice to place confidence in God and His Word. Unbelief is a sin because it is a deliberate choice to withhold confidence in God and His Word.

Faith is a receiving of the truth, an embracing of the truth, a commitment to the truth—and to the God of truth! And commitment always produces action. That is why faith without works is dead (James 2:17). With no action there is no commitment. With no commitment there is no faith!

So what is faith? The scriptural definition of faith is given in **Hebrews 11:1**: *"Now faith is the substance of things hoped for, the evidence of things not seen" (NKJV).*

Biblical faith contains two elements: substance and evidence. The term substance is a good translation of the Greek term used in Hebrews 11:1, which literally means *"that which has real existence, or the substance of something."* Therefore, your individual faith is something real that does in fact have an existence. In the eighth grade, when I took my first algebra course, I had a math teacher who was usually very helpful. During the first couple of weeks, I did not understand the basics of algebra. I finally raised my hand in class to get an explanation.

I wanted to know where he got the x and y in the equation. Instead of answering, he reached up into the air, grabbed a fistful, and pulled it down to the blackboard where he had written the equation. After doing it a few times without speaking, after my face had turned a thousand shades of red, he finally explained to us that the x and y of the equation were just "placeholders" to serve in place until the final answer appeared in the equation.

### Mark 11:24

*"Therefore I tell you, whatever you ask for in prayer, believe that you have already received it, and it will be yours."*

This Scripture shows us that by faith you can claim a promise that God makes to you in His Word. If you believe that you have received the answer when you pray (Mark 11:24), then your faith stands in the place of what you ask for until it is manifested visibly to the natural eye. Everything always exists in the spiritual before it becomes visible to the natural eye. God first envisioned the universe before He spoke it into existence. Your faith takes the place of what you ask for as an invisible, but nevertheless very real substance until the thing you claim is made visible to your natural sight. At that point your faith is then no longer needed for that particular prayer request.

### Faith Is Substance

Faith is the substance of things hoped for. It is as real in the sight of God, as the thing for which you asked will be real to you when you see it manifested to the natural eye. Your faith is the exact image of that which you ask for. It is like looking in the mirror at the result of your prayer petition. As an image it is but the reflection of the actuality or reality. So when faith is present, it can only mean one thing—that the things you have asked for are yours and only await their manifestation by God in His own time!

### Faith Is Evidence

Faith is also evidence. Faith is the evidence of things not seen. Evidence of anything is absolute proof of its reality and existence. This means that the very fact that you have faith that God has heard and granted your request is evidence that you have already received what you do not yet see. You have received it "by faith." You now are able to see the invisible become reality with the spiritual eye of faith. When you sense and know in your heart and spirit that your request has been answered before you see it, your faith is the evidence that you indeed will have it.

Faith is believing God. Faith is simply taking God at His Word! Faith is saying to God, "Here's my life...I trust that You know what is best for me!" Contrary to some thinking, faith is not in any way a passive state of being. It is an active work based upon a spiritual knowledge of possibilities that result in action. Faith produces: results, miracles, salvation, spiritual living, contact with God, healing, answers to our prayers, renewal, etc. These things are not the product of some mental action manufactured within a passive state of mind. These things come by prayer and faith in God.

We believe God not because we see miracles. We see miracles because we believe God. And we believe God on the basis of His own self-revelation. So seeing does not produce believing; but rather believing produces seeing.

Answered prayer strengthens faith, but faith cannot be based on answered prayer. Faith is based on the God who answers prayer.

In the eleventh chapter of Hebrews, the Bible presents the characteristics of real faith. It tells us about faith not by giving an abstract analysis, but by demonstrating faith in action in the lives of some of the great men and women of faith.

So in Hebrews 11, we see faith in action, and in the action we see revealed the various elements or characteristics of real faith. Let's look briefly at some of them. In verse 3 we read, "Through faith we understand that the worlds were framed by the word of God."

How the material universe came into existence is a question beyond science. It is a matter of faith, and true faith understands it happened by the word of God. Verse 4 says that Abel offered to God a more excellent sacrifice, a blood sacrifice. True faith always approaches God by the "more excellent sacrifice," the blood of Jesus. In verse 5 we are informed that by faith Enoch was translated because he pleased God. There is no faith without a life that pleases God, and only by a life of faith can we please God.

Verse 6 says that diligence in seeking God is one of the principles of faith. God is not a vending machine. We do not always get the answer the moment we pray. God is working out His purpose in us, and He works in the process of time. When we seek God diligently, we give Him a chance to do something that He has really been wanting to do in us all along. Don't give up. Demonstrate to God that you mean business. The answer is yours, and it will come. And when the answer comes, you may discover that in the process of diligent prayer, you received something far more valuable than the thing itself for which you were praying.

Verse 7 says that by faith, Noah prepared an ark. Faith prepares for the answer. When you pray, make room for the blessing. Verse

8 testifies that by faith, Abraham "obeyed; and he went out, not knowing whither he went." Faith obeys. Faith and obedience cannot be separated. Faith is obedient confidence, and it is confident obedience. Faith is a surrender to the whole truth.

Faith cannot take the promises of God seriously while ignoring His instructions. Faith takes God seriously in everything He has spoken, in His commandments as well as His promises. So a faith that refuses to obey is no faith at all. If it disregards the truth, it is dead. Faith obeys the will of God without foreseeing all the consequences of its trusting commitment. It sees the path of truth and plants its feet firmly therein. Abraham did not know where he was going, but he knew that he was on the right road. Verse 17 says: "By faith Abraham, when he was tried, offered up Isaac." Of course this was not the only time Abraham was tried, but it probably was his most outstanding trial.

Here was the situation. God had promised to make Abraham a father of many nations and to bless all nations through his seed. This was to happen through a line descending through Isaac. Then God commanded Abraham to offer up Isaac as a burnt offering. Most folk in Abraham's situation would immediately become confused, their faith smashed. "Has God changed His mind? Has He gone back on His word? Can it be that the immutable, changeless God has failed?"

Not so with Abraham. Though the "contradictions" seemed irreconcilable, the questions unanswerable, though the whole thing did not compute, there is no record that Abraham's faith faltered or that he hesitated for a minute. Abraham proceeded without question or complaint. Why? Because Abraham knew the God he served! Abraham had settled some things in his heart about the character of God: God is alive; God is just; God is faithful; God knows what He is doing and why He is doing it. Abraham knew that if he continued in the process to sacrifice Isaac, which God ultimately did not permit him to do, God would still be faithful.

If our faith is steadfast and victorious, we will be like Abraham. We will place absolute confidence in the character of God. We must settle some things in our hearts about God. We all go through circumstances that we do not understand. We don't know why God allows this or that. In these times, we can either say that God failed and charge Him with folly, or we can confess His faithfulness and declare, "I'm going to hold to God's unchanging hand and trust in Him though I don't understand!"

This kind of victorious, overcoming faith is not gained overnight. It is not built by careless, half-hearted Christian living or by being saved one day and backslidden the next. No, it comes by walking consistently and faithfully with God day in and day out, year after year!

And then there was Moses. Read about him in verses 23 through 28. Moses exemplifies another essential ingredient of overcoming, victorious faith—a proper sense of external values. Anyone who thinks he or she has opportunities to live it up should take a look at Moses. In the court of Egypt, as the adopted son of Pharaoh's daughter, Moses had every means at his disposal to achieve total self-indulgence.

But Moses took one look at the whole thing and made a value decision. He said in effect, "I don't care what Egypt has to offer. I'll take the reproach of Christ instead. That's worth more than all the pleasures and treasures in Egypt!" Real faith makes an external value decision. If we are to be stable, overcoming Christians, we must settle in our hearts once and for all that Jesus Christ is worth more than the whole world and live accordingly!

Faith means action, as noted in Hebrews chapter 11. Through faith…worlds were framed, Abel offered, Enoch went up, Noah moved, Abraham went out, Sarah received, Moses refused and forsook, Rahab lived. All of this was done by active faith! We are the children of this kind of faith, which was brought to us by the patriarchs of the Old Testament. Our own spiritual birth came solely and only by faith. We must be convinced, to the point of risking everything, that God is not only able, but also willing to perform those things He has promised to do.

Romans 4:18–21 states that Abraham was fully persuaded that God was able to perform, or bring to pass, what He had promised to us. Abraham considered not his own body, now as good as dead, staggered not at the promise, was strong in faith, was fully persuaded. When God told Abraham that Sarah would bring forth a son, it was physically impossible for Sarah to bear a child.

Yet this made no difference to Abraham. When told that a son would be born, he accepted this as though it were normal. What the world looks at as different, such as supernatural healings, conversions, and other miracles, should be the normal or expected thing around us.

This is simply "considering not" the circumstances. Faith is simply "considering not" the circumstances and looking beyond the surroundings and the natural reasons as to why it can't happen to God, who calls things "which be not as though they were." When God speaks to you, believe it! Have faith in God and trust Him!

Luke 1 tells the story of Zacharias, a man who prayed but didn't believe. Zacharias and Elisabeth prayed all the time that God would give them a child. A lot of years had slipped by, and they were close to ninety years of age, certainly past childbearing age. But Zacharias was a religious man, the kind who is used to praying but not getting any answers. And he had done it for years.

One day he was standing before God's altar when the angel of the Lord appeared to him and he got scared, which tells you that there is a lot of difference between ritual and reality. But the angel of God said, "Zacharias, your prayers have been heard. I am going to give you a son."

Zacharias said, "You can't do that. What do you mean, give us a son? Why Lizzie and I are too old!" God said to Zacharias, "Well, you'll still get your son, Zack, but you're not going to talk till it happens because you did not believe Me!" After that, Zacharias went around writing instead of talking for nearly nine months.

Noah is an example of faith with works, or obedient faith. Genesis 6:5 tells the story. According to the Scriptures, he was the only man in the family who found favor in the eyes of the Lord. When God announced an event unprecedented in Noah's experience, Noah simply believed God. He showed that he believed by preparing for the day when God's pronouncement would come true.

Life in Noah's day had deteriorated from Eden's innocent beauty. In an age when people disregarded God, Noah was an example of obedient faith. God first gave the reason to build the ark: coming floods of destruction. Then He gave the direction to build the ark. Noah first walked with God; then he received specific instructions.

Faith requires risk. God's direction to Noah was ridiculous in man's eyes. Noah had never seen an ark, much less built one on dry land. He was required to take two risks. The first was to believe that destruction was coming. Outwardly life seemed normal. People were eating, drinking, marrying, and divorcing. God frowned on this and decided to destroy the world.

The second risk Noah took was to believe that an ark would indeed provide salvation. Even though Noah had never seen an ark, nor had there been a flood to ever require that size of boat, he believed both. Faith requires action! And Noah went to work. He invested all of his efforts for 120 years or so, with absolutely no response from God. None! No rain, no flood.

If we really believe that God is going to do what He has said, a lot of preparation is required of us. But with Noah, his heart was right toward God. He was a covenant man with a covenant family. He was an example to his wife and his sons. His sons, in turn, had apparently been an example to their wives, for their families were intact. They were walking in the ways of God in the midst of a disintegrating society.

But it takes a long time to build. Scripture says that after Noah started building the ark, it was over a hundred years before he got in the thing. What patience he must have had. But a hundred years later, when it started to rain, Noah's boat was ready. Now, wouldn't it have been sad if Noah had waited fifty years before starting the hundred-year task God had given him? The point is this: It takes as long as God says it takes to do what God says must be done. Now is the time for preparation!

Our preparation is evidence of our faith. If you believe the Scriptures, the evidence that you believe is preparation. It is foolish for us to testify that we believe God will do a mighty work in the earth, that the knowledge of the Lord will cover the earth as the waters cover the sea...and make no preparation. Because preparation is the evidence of faith.

You may be thinking, But my faith is weak. Can you imagine someone saying that there is no sun in the sky because they can't hear it? Or can you imagine someone saying that there is no wind because they can't see it? Some want to hear what they can't hear with their natural ears and see what they can't see with their natural eyes. The Lord went out of His way to get Thomas to believe. He said to Thomas, "Put your hand over here...feel these scars." Anybody can believe this way! But Jesus said, "Blessed is he that has not seen, and yet believed!" In other words, blessed is the man that sees by faith something in the invisible world and holds on to it by faith until it appears in the natural world. God's Word is eternal. Heaven and earth may pass away, but God's Word will still be the same.

### Luke 5:17–26

*"And when he saw their faith..."*

My challenge to all readers of this book is for you to open your eyes to the invisible world of faith.

### Mark 11:24

*"Therefore I tell you, whatever you ask for in prayer, believe that you have already received it, and it will be yours."*

**Deuteronomy 7:9**

*"Therefore know that the Lord your God, He is God, the faithful God who keeps covenant and mercy for a thousand generations with those who love Him and keep His commandments." (NKJV)*

**John 14:13–14**

*"And whatever you ask in My name, that I will do, that the Father may be glorified in the Son. If you ask anything in My name, I will do it." (NKJV)*

**1 Corinthians 2:5**

*"That your faith should not stand in the wisdom of men, but in the power of God."*

**John 20:1–13**

*"The first day of the week cometh Mary Magdalene early, when it was yet dark, unto the sepulchre, and seeth the stone taken away from the sepulchre. Then she runneth, and cometh to Simon Peter, and to the other disciple, whom Jesus loved, and saith unto them, They have taken away the Lord out of the sepulchre, and we know not where they have laid him. Peter therefore went forth, and that other disciple, and came to the sepulchre. So they ran both together: and the other disciple did outrun Peter, and came first to the sepulchre. And he stooping down, and looking in, saw the linen clothes lying; yet went he not in.*

*Then cometh Simon Peter following him, and went into the sepulchre, and seeth the linen clothes lie, and the napkin, that was about his head, not lying with the linen clothes, but wrapped together in a place by itself. Then went in also that other disciple, which came first to the sepulchre, and he saw, and believed. For as yet they knew not the scripture, that he must rise again from the dead. Then the disciples went away again unto their own home. But Mary stood without at the sepulchre weeping: and as she wept, she stooped down, and looked into the sepulchre, And seeth two angels in white sitting, the one at the head, and the other at the feet, where the body of Jesus had lain. And they say unto her, Woman, why weepest thou? She saith unto them, Because they have taken away my Lord, and I know not where they have laid him." (KJV)*

This is a story about people who had quit and were going home! Two men and a woman are the main characters. The men had been partners in the fishing business, and the woman—well, the Bible simply states that before she met Jesus, she had been controlled by demons. Her name was Mary Magdalene; the men were Peter and John. Now it was the morning of the Resurrection. First, at the tomb of Christ, Mary discovered that the body was gone and ran to tell Peter and John. They in turn ran back with Mary to the grave. Excitement was everywhere. Everybody in the story is running! This is typical of those who have just discovered the supernatural element in Christianity.

Because the disciples had been following Jesus, you might say that these men had been going to church every day for the past three and a half years. But this was the first time a miracle of this magnitude had ever occurred. So they got all excited and ran! Peter and John ran to the grave, looked in, and saw nothing—that is, nothing except some grave clothes and a napkin. John 20:10 states they "went away again unto their own home." All of that running for nothing.

A brief summary of John 20 is this: The two men (Peter and John) saw nothing. They gave up too soon. But Mary waited outside the tomb and saw the angels.

Sometimes we need to do some waiting.

### Psalm 37:7

*"Rest in the Lord, and wait patiently for him."*

### Isaiah 40:31

*"But they that wait upon the Lord shall renew their strength; they shall mount up with wings as eagles; they shall run, and not be weary; and they shall walk, and not faint."*

### Galatians 6:9

*"And let us not be weary in well doing: for in due season we shall reap, if we faint not." (KJV)*

Sometimes we need to persevere.

### Ephesians 6:18

*"Praying always with all prayer and supplication in the Spirit, and watching thereunto with all perseverance and supplication for all saints."*

Sometimes we need some endurance.

### Matthew 24:13

*"But he that shall endure unto the end, the same shall be saved."*

### Hebrews 6:15

*"And so, after he (Abraham) had patiently endured, he obtained the promise."*

Sometimes we need to have diligence and patience!

### Hebrews 6:10–12

*"For God is not unrighteous to forget your work and labour of love, which ye have shewed toward his name, in that ye have ministered to the saints, and do minister. And we desire that every one of you do shew the same diligence to the full assurance of hope unto the end: That ye be not slothful, but followers of them who through faith and patience inherit the promises." (KJV)*

How will the desired result come? How will we see the promise come to us? Through faith and patience!

### Hebrews 10:35–36

*"Therefore, do not throw away your confidence, which has a great reward. (nasb) For ye have need of patience, that, after ye have done the will of God, ye might receive the promise." (KJV)*

So Mary waited outside the tomb. When the two men had gone, she looked inside—and saw what they did not see. She heard what they did not hear. Two angels were in that "empty" tomb! Now there is nothing in the story to indicate that the angels came especially to meet Mary. They were probably there for Peter and John too. The difference lay in the awareness of the disciples. Some of us are just not as tuned into the spiritual world as others. All of us know that there are two worlds. But we are tuned in to the material world. Our five senses provide continuous information about our surroundings. So we see an empty grave and some funeral clothes and often miss what God is saying to each of us. When we see problems all around us, we often worry.

When we see trouble all around, we often despair. When we see confusion surrounding us, we often get discouraged. But try to hone your spiritual eyes and ears, as Mary did, and recognize that in spite of what our human eyes see, God is at work in the spiritual world! What have you asked God for? What are you believing for in faith? What about that element of faith will bring into your life the supernatural provision you have been seeking?

### John 14:13

*"And whatsoever ye shall ask in my name, that will I do, that the Father may be glorified in the Son." (KJV)*

### John 14:14

*"If ye shall ask any thing in my name, I will do it." (KJV)*

### John 16:23

*"And in that day ye shall ask me nothing. Verily, verily, I say*

unto you, Whatsoever ye shall ask the Father in my name, he will give it you." (KJV)

### John 16:24

"Hitherto have ye asked nothing in my name: ask, and ye shall receive, that your joy may be full." (KJV)

# The Principle of
# Grounding Your Faith in the Word

**Romans 10:17** *"…cometh by hearing"*

**Matthew 6:33** *"…seek ye first"*

**James 5:15–18** *"      …prayer of faith"*

**Numbers 23:19** *"…God is not a man that he should lie"*

## Romans 10:17-18

*"Consequently, faith comes from hearing the message, and the message is heard through the word of Christ. But I ask: Did they not hear? Of course they did: 'Their voice has gone out into all the earth, their words to the ends of the world.'"*

## Matthew 6:33

*"But seek first his kingdom and his righteousness, and all these things will be given to you as well."*

## James 5:15-18

*"And the prayer offered in faith will make the sick person well; the Lord will raise him up. If he has sinned, he will be forgiven. 16 Therefore confess your sins to each other and pray for each other so that you may be healed. The prayer of a righteous man is powerful and effective. Elijah was a man just like us. He prayed earnestly that it would not rain, and it did not rain on the land for three and a half years. Again he prayed, and the heavens gave rain, and the earth produced its crops."*

**Numbers 23:19**

*"God is not a man, that he should lie, nor a son of man, that he should change his mind. Does he speak and then not act? Does he promise and not fulfill?"*

# *The Principle of Claiming Your Faith*

Claim as yours what your faith has embraced from the Word.

**Matthew 7:7–11** *"…ask, seek, knock"*

The promises of God are not fulfilled merely because we believe them; we receive only what we specifically claim as ours by faith. It is not ours until we appropriate it by faith. This is very clear in reference to salvation. God promises salvation to all, but it doesn't happen apart from your personally asking for it.

**James 4:2–3** *"…you have not, because you ask not"*

When you ask, do it in simple, childlike faith. Faith does not plead and beg for what God has promised. This would indicate a lack of faith. If we think we have to persuade God to do what He has already offered to do for those who ask, we simply are not asking in faith.

**Matthew 21:22** *"…ask specifically in prayer"*

**Corinthians 1:20** *"…yea and amen"*

---

# *The Principle of*
# *Confessing Your Faith*

Boldly confess what you have believed and claimed by faith.

Confession is faith's way of expressing itself.

> ***Romans 10:10*** *"…with the mouth confession is made" unto salvation"*

If we really believe that God will keep His promise to us, it will be expressed by what we say or confess. We receive what we confess by faith. This is why Scripture places such a strong emphasis upon confession.

> ***Matthew 10:32–33*** *"…confess me before men"*
>
> ***I Timothy 6:12*** *"…fight the good fight of faith"*
>
> ***James 1:6–7*** *"…ask in faith, nothing wavering"*

If we make a negative confession of doubt, then we receive nothing. If we confess what God's Word says, then He will bring it to pass. There is something to a confident belief without doubting. If, for example, you claim a promise and later begin to express doubt and anxiety because it is not manifested immediately, your condition may never rise above the level of your faith and confession.

Confession of doubt seems to imprison your faith so that it cannot be released. Proverbs 6:2 talks about being snared or trapped by the words of our mouth. If your confession does not agree with God's Word, then it is not faith speaking! Faith always agrees with God's Word.

This is the literal meaning of the verb "to confess" in the New Testament Greek. Homologeo means "to agree with, to speak the same language, to confess."

# *The Principle of*
# *Acting on Your Faith*

**J**ames 2:17 says, *"Faith, if it hath not works, is dead."* John 9:7 talks about when Jesus anointed the blind man's eyes with clay and commanded him to go wash in the pool of Siloam. This gave the man an opportunity to put his faith into action.

In Mark 2:1–12, Jesus saw the faith of the men who lowered the sick man down through the roof. It seems obvious that Jesus noticed their faith at work, when it notes in verse 5 that He saw their faith. This shows us an example of faith in action!

So faith is not just some mind-set or intangible thing. It is an act. Much like grace. Grace is more than just unmerited favor, or the fact that we have received something from God that we do not deserve. Grace is God's operational activity in our daily lives. All the heroes of faith recorded in the eleventh chapter of Hebrews are said to have done something that gave evidence of their faith.

When we are truly activating our God given faith, we will act upon it. If you claim a promise of God, you may not know the exact moment the manifestation will occur, but it always comes as you are acting in agreement with your confession of faith in God's Word. It will never come in the midst of doubt or failure to act on your faith.

## The Principle of
## Holding Fast Without Wavering

Hold fast to your confession of faith without wavering. Sometimes people seek to appropriate a promise of God by faith. They claim His promise and confess it, but if it is not manifested immediately, or soon after they have petitioned God, they find that they cannot maintain a positive confession of faith in God's promise, and thus they do not receive the manifestation of their promise.

Read Matthew 14:22–32, which talks about Peter walking on the water. **Hebrews 10:23** says, *"Let us hold fast the profession of our faith without wavering: for he is faithful that promised."* **James 1:6** notes, *"But let him ask in faith, nothing wavering...like a wave."* **Romans 4:17** declares, *"Even God, who quickeneth the dead, and calleth those things which be not as though they were."* Here is what **Mark 11:22–24** observes: *"Have faith in God...what things soever ye desire...believe that ye receive them...and ye shall have them."*

In John 9, the blind man's healing was not manifested immediately. He had some things to do first. It was not until after he had washed (Jesus said to "go wash") that he came to see. The ten lepers of Luke 17:12–14 did not receive the manifestation of their healing when they asked, or immediately after Jesus granted their petition. According to Scripture, they were healed "as they went." Verse 14 says, "And it came to pass, that, as they went they were cleansed."

According to **Romans 4:17–21**, Abraham waited many years for the manifestation of God's promise to him—the promise of a son—while holding fast to his faith without doubting.

**Verse 19** *"...and being not weak in faith"*

**Verse 20** *"…but was strong in faith"*

**Verse 21** *"…and being fully persuaded"*

Our confession is not based on what we see, what we feel, or what outward circumstances seem to indicate. Our confession of faith is based solely on what God says has been done for us when we pray. Once you have claimed by faith a promise of God, continuing to beg Him is to lack in faith. Even though the manifestation is not seen as yet by our natural eyes, give thanks to God for hearing your petition, knowing that His answer is on the way.

The Bible says that God "watches over His Word to perform it." John 1:1 says, "In the beginning was the Word and the Word was with God and the Word was God." God spoke the words of the Bible, God is behind every word, and God watches over every promise to make it good.

Jesus said in **Mark 9:23**, *"Everything is possible for him who believes"*—if you believe!

## *The Principle of Hope in God*

*1 Timothy 6:17–18*

*"But to put their hope in God, who richly provides us with everything for our enjoyment."*

Probably no one reading this book is concerned about whether or not he or she will have food to eat today. And for that matter few will be concerned about eating tomorrow or the next day. Most citizens of developed nations do not have to worry about their next meal. In some cities there is poverty, clothing needs occur, more shelters are needed for the homeless, and other needs may arise. But this Scripture says that when we trust in God, He will provide for us. We may not have the means to purchase food, clothing, and shelter, but one of God's children does. The following story is of one such servant.

It was a blistery day in New York City. It's frigid in December. A nine-year-old lad was standing before a shoe store on Broadway, barefooted, peering through the window and shivering with cold. A lady approached the boy and said, "My little fellow, why are you looking so intently in that window?" "I was asking God to give me a pair of shoes," the boy replied. The lady took him by the hand and went into the store and asked the clerk to get a half-dozen pairs of socks for the boy. She then asked if the clerk could give her a bucket of water and a towel. He quickly brought them to her.

She took the little fellow to the back part of the store and, removing her gloves, knelt down, washed his little feet, and dried them with a towel. By this time the clerk had returned with the socks. Placing a pair upon the boy's feet, she then purchased him a pair of shoes, bagged up the remaining socks, and gave them to him. She patted him on the head and said, "No doubt, young man, you feel more comfortable now?" As she turned to go, the astonished lad caught her by the hand and, looking up in her face, with tears in his eyes, answered the question with these words: "Are you God's wife?"

(Source Unknown)

Your circumstances may change through different seasons of your life, but if your hope is in God, your needs will always be supplied.

# The Principle of
# Sowing and Reaping

Some events seem to be a way of life. For example, you never get a busy signal when you dial a wrong number. Children never seem to spill their food on dirty floors, and the line at the grocery store is always the longest when you are in a hurry.

It seems that while waiting in line at the bank, the gas station, or the grocery store, the other line next to you moves faster. I was in a local variety store in Portland, Oregon, by the name of Fred Meyer. While headed for the "10 items or less" line, an entire family cut just in front of me. I was in a hurry, but waited until they all crowded into line in front of me. Their cart was filled with grocery items. As I watched in surprise, the parents passed out money to the kids and proceeded to divide up the cart between themselves and the kids.

Additional weird principles might include: It always rains on the weekends, you seem to get sick on your day off, etc. Perhaps they could be called "Murphy's Other Laws." Some of these laws you can live without knowing about. However, there are some laws you ignore at your own risk and potential destruction.

There are basic laws of nature. The law of living is giving. If money is to be useful, it must be used. In the law of sowing and reaping: here are some things to consider:

**1. The seed we plant is the same kind of seed we reap— seed of its kind.**

One phenomenon of God's creation is that seed we plant is from the fruit that was harvested. We see this in life. Parents often see in their children the characteristics of themselves, good and bad. Each of us must set good examples, for life is spent planting. You have no choice but to sow. When we sow financial seeds into God's kingdom, we benefit from the same.

## 2. We determine the size of the harvest at the time of planting. (2 Corinthians 9:6, 8, 11)

The farmer who plants hundreds or thousands of acres knows that, barring some natural disaster, he is going to reap more than he planted, but always in proportion to what he planted. One who is generous with his time, talents, and resources is going to reap generously. One who is generous with love, appreciation, and mercy will reap in the proportion he sows those qualities.

The man who gives beyond his tithe (the tithe belongs to the Lord) has just begun to give. The more one gives, the more one reaps. But don't just look for repayment in monetary measure. Good health is more important than money. A family serving the Lord is more important than dollars.

## 3. We will always have a harvest. (Malachi 3:10; Galatians 6:9)

No one has ever experienced crop failure. This law is as sure as the rising and setting of the sun. The success of this harvest is not determined by natural laws, but is governed by the Lord Himself. Should you sow your seed into your local place of worship where you and your family receive much benefit? Of course! Will you reap the harvest? Certainly! You and your family reap a good harvest every time your local pastor preaches the Word and sows good seed into your life.

## 4. You will usually reap later than you sow.

In the American Midwest, farms are everywhere. You don't have to be around a farm too long to learn that both growth and decay take time. The same is true in our spiritual lives. Perhaps this is the reason Paul warned that we shouldn't be deceived. There's a caution in sowing to the flesh. Nothing seems to happen right away. Marriages do not collapse in an instant. Walking away from right things usually doesn't happen overnight. People become deceived and don't realize what's happening until they are trapped.

While we receive much immediate benefit when we sow into our local church, it doesn't stop there. We continue to reap the harvest throughout our lives because the seed continues to multiply.

### 5. We will always reap more than we planted. (Matthew 13:8)

When we plant a kernel of corn, we reap a stalk with several ears of corn on it. On the ears of corn are hundreds of kernels. So it is with a blade of wheat. Only God could design such a wonder. The law of increased return is what makes farming a workable business enterprise. But sowing to the Spirit results in eternal life. First Corinthians 2:9 says, "No eye has seen, no ear has heard, no mind conceived, what God has prepared for those who love him."

### 6. There is a season for planting and a season for harvesting. (Ecclesiastes 3:1–2)

Not all harvesting follows immediately. The time element is important. If the seed germinates before its proper time, a harvest can be lost. Many give as if there will not be a harvest. Some people think God has not noted what they are planting simply because they have not experienced a harvest. But if we plant the seed, a harvest will come. For example, consider Proverbs 22:6: "Train a child in the way he should go, and when he is old he will not turn from it." The promise is that if we continue to plant the seed of godly training when the child is young, then in a different season of life the child will not forget his training. Thus as parents or grandparents we enjoy the harvest, even though it might be years later.

### 7. Seed can be sown secretly; however, the harvest is always viewed by many.

We do not see or hear all the work, sweat, and tears that a person has expended to plant the seed. It may seem to those who did not have to do it that it was just yesterday. But in time, the farmer will see the golden fields being blown by the wind.

**8. We are responsible to sow and God is responsible for the harvest.**

We are laborers together with God. God does not produce failures; He is the Lord of the harvest. With these laws God has set in order, we need to sow seed that is going to bring fruit both now and for eternity. He is the Lord of the harvest. As we enter each new season, we must start by planting.

# The Principle of
# Understanding the Greatest Blessing

### Acts 20:34–35

*"In everything I did, I showed you that by this kind of hard work we must help the weak, remembering the words the Lord Jesus himself said: 'It is more blessed to give than to receive.'"*

No doubt you have already learned this principle and practiced it for years. Truly it is a greater blessing to give to others than it is to receive from others. The following story illustrates the principle of the greatest blessing.

Young Nathaniel was getting cold sitting out in his backyard in the snow. Nathaniel didn't wear boots—he didn't like them and anyway he didn't own any. The thin sneakers he wore had a few holes in them, and they did a poor job of keeping out the cold. Nathaniel had been in his backyard for about an hour already, and try as he might, he could not come up with an idea for his mother's Christmas gift. He shook his head as he thought, This is useless. Even if I do come up with an idea, I don't have any money to spend.

Ever since his father had passed away a year before, the family of five had struggled. It wasn't because his mother didn't care or try; there just never seemed to be enough. She worked nights at the hospital, but the small wage she was earning could only be stretched so far. What the family lacked in money and material things, they more than made up for in love and family unity. Nathaniel had two older sisters who ran the household in their mother's absence. Both of his sisters had already made beautiful gifts for their mother. Somehow it just wasn't fair. Here it was Christmas Eve already, and he had nothing.

Wiping a tear from his eye, Nathaniel kicked the snow and started to walk down to the street where the shops and stores were. It wasn't easy being seven without a father, especially when he needed a man to talk to. Nathaniel walked from shop to shop, looking into each decorated window. Everything seemed so beautiful and so out of reach. It was starting to get dark and Nathaniel reluctantly turned to walk home, when suddenly his eyes caught the glimmer of the setting sun's rays reflecting off something along the curb. He reached down and discovered a shiny dime. Never before has anyone felt so wealthy as Nathaniel felt at that moment. As he held his newfound treasure, a warmth spread throughout his entire body, and he walked into the first store he saw. His excitement quickly turned cold when salesperson after salesperson told him that he could not buy anything with only a dime.

He saw a flower shop and went inside to wait in line. When the shop owner asked if he could help him, Nathaniel presented the dime and asked if he could buy one flower for his mother's Christmas gift. The shop owner looked at Nathaniel and his ten cent offering. Then he put his hand on Nathaniel's shoulder and said to him, *"You just wait here, and I'll see what I can do for you."*

As Nathaniel waited, he looked at the beautiful flowers, and even though he was a boy, he could see why mothers and girls liked flowers.

The sound of the door closing as the last customer left jolted Nathaniel back to reality. All alone in the shop, he began to feel alone and afraid. Suddenly the shop owner came out and moved to the counter. There, before Nathaniel's eyes, lay twelve long stem red roses, with leaves of green and tiny white flowers all tied together with a big silver bow. Nathaniel's heart sank as the owner picked them up and placed them gently into a long white box. *"That will be ten cents young man,"* the shop owner said, reaching out his hand for the dime. Slowly, Nathaniel moved his hand to give the man his dime. Could this be true? No one else would give him a thing for his dime! Sensing the boy's reluctance, the shop owner added, *"I just happened to have some roses on sale for ten cents a dozen. Would you like them?"*

This time Nathaniel did not hesitate, and when the man placed the long box into his hands, he knew it was true. Walking out the door that the owner was holding for Nathaniel, he heard the shopkeeper say, *"Merry Christmas, young man."*

As he returned inside, the shopkeeper's wife walked out. "Who were you talking to back there, and where are the roses you were fixing?"

Staring out the window and blinking the tears from his eyes, he replied, *"A strange thing happened to me this morning. While I was setting up things to open the shop, I thought I heard a voice telling me to set aside a dozen of my best roses for a special gift. I wasn't sure at the time whether I had lost my mind or what, but I set them aside anyway. Then just a few minutes ago, a little boy came into the shop and wanted to buy a flower for his mother with one small dime."*

*"When I looked at him, I saw myself, many years ago. I, too, was a poor boy with nothing to buy my mother a Christmas gift. A bearded man, whom I never knew, stopped me on the street and told me that he wanted to give me ten dollars."*

*"When I saw that little boy tonight, I knew who that voice was, and I put together a dozen of my very best roses."*

The shop owner and his wife hugged each other tightly, and as they stepped out into the bitter cold air, they somehow didn't feel cold at all.

(Source Unknown)

# The Principle of
# *Knowing the Faithfulness of God*

Scriptural Passages About the Faithfulness of God

### Deuteronomy 32:4

*"He is the Rock, his works are perfect, and all his ways are just. A faithful God who does no wrong, upright and just is he."*

### Deuteronomy 7:9

*"Therefore know that the Lord your God, He is God, the faithful God who keeps covenant and mercy for a thousand generations with those who love Him and keep His commandments." (NKJV)*

### Psalm 145:13

*"Your kingdom is an everlasting kingdom, and your dominion endures through all generations. The Lord is faithful to all his promises and loving toward all he has made."*

### Isaiah 55:3

*"Give ear and come to me; hear me, that your soul may live. I will make an everlasting covenant with you, my faithful love promised to David."*

### I Corinthians 1:9

*"God is faithful, by whom you were called into the fellowship of His Son, Jesus Christ our Lord." (NKJV)*

### I Corinthians 10:13

*"No temptation has overtaken you except such as is common to man; but God is faithful, who will not allow you to*

be tempted beyond what you are able, but with the temptation will also make the way of escape, that you may be able to bear it." (NKJV)

### 2 Corinthians 1:18

"But as God is faithful, our word to you was not Yes and No." (NKJV)

### 2 Thessalonians 3:3

"But the Lord is faithful, who will establish you and guard you from the evil one." (NKJV)

### Hebrew 3:6

"But Christ is faithful as a son over God's house. And we are his house, if we hold on to our courage and the hope of which we boast."

### Hebrew 11:11

"By faith Sarah herself also received strength to conceive seed, and she bore a child when she was past the age, because she judged Him faithful who had promised." (NKJV)

### 1 Peter 4:19

"Therefore let those who suffer according to the will of God commit their souls to Him in doing good, as to a faithful Creator." (NKJV)

### 1 John 1:9

"If we confess our sins, He is faithful and just to forgive us our sins and to cleanse us from all unrighteousness." (NKJV)

Scriptural Passages About Faith

### Matthew 6:30

"If that is how God clothes the grass of the field, which is here today and tomorrow is thrown into the fire, will he not much more clothe you, O you of little faith?"

### Matthew 8:10

*"When Jesus heard this, he was astonished and said to those following him, 'I tell you the truth, I have not found anyone in Israel with such great faith.'"*

### Matthew 8:26

*"He replied, 'You of little faith, why are you so afraid?'" Then he got up and rebuked the winds and the waves, and it was completely calm."*

### Matthew 9:2

*"Some men brought to him a paralytic, lying on a mat. When Jesus saw their faith, he said to the paralytic, 'Take heart, son; your sins are forgiven.'"*

### Matthew 9:22

*"Jesus turned and saw her. 'Take heart, daughter,' he said, 'your faith has healed you.' And the woman was healed from that moment."*

### Matthew 9:29

*"Then he touched their eyes and said, 'According to your faith will it be done to you.'"*

### Matthew 14:31

*"Immediately Jesus reached out his hand and caught him. 'You of little faith,' he said, 'why did you doubt?'"*

### Matthew 15:28

*"Then Jesus answered, 'Woman, you have great faith! Your request is granted.' And her daughter was healed from that very hour."*

### Matthew 16:8

*"Aware of their discussion, Jesus asked, 'You of little faith, why are you talking among yourselves about having no bread?'"*

### Matthew 17:20

"He replied, 'Because you have so little faith. I tell you the truth, if you have faith as small as a mustard seed, you can say to this mountain, 'Move from here to there' and it will move. Nothing will be impossible for you.'"

### Matthew 21:21

"Jesus replied, 'I tell you the truth, if you have faith and do not doubt, not only can you do what was done to the fig tree, but also you can say to this mountain, 'Go, throw yourself into the sea,' and it will be done.'"

### Mark 2:5

"When Jesus saw their faith, he said to the paralytic, 'Son, your sins are forgiven.'"

### Mark 4:40

"He said to his disciples, 'Why are you so afraid? Do you still have no faith?'"

### Mark 5:34

"He said to her, 'Daughter, your faith has healed you. Go in peace and be freed from your suffering.'"

### Mark 10:52

"'Go,' said Jesus, 'your faith has healed you.' Immediately he received his sight and followed Jesus along the road."

### Mark 11:22

"Have faith in God,' Jesus answered.'"

### Luke 5:20

"When Jesus saw their faith, he said, 'Friend, your sins are forgiven.'"

### Luke 7:9

"When Jesus heard this, he was amazed at him, and turning to the crowd following him, he said, 'I tell you, I have not found such great faith even in Israel.'"

**Luke 7:50**

*"Jesus said to the woman, 'Your faith has saved you; go in peace.'"*

**Luke 8:25**

*"Where is your faith?" he asked his disciples. In fear and amazement they asked one another, 'Who is this? He commands even the winds and the water, and they obey him.'"*

**Luke 8:48**

*"Then he said to her, 'Daughter, your faith has healed you. Go in peace.'"*

**Luke 12:28**

*"If that is how God clothes the grass of the field, which is here today, and tomorrow is thrown into the fire, how much more will he clothe you, O you of little faith!"*

**Luke 17:5**

*"The apostles said to the Lord, 'Increase our faith!'"*

**Luke 17:6**

*"He replied, 'If you have faith as small as a mustard seed, you can say to this mulberry tree, 'Be uprooted and planted in the sea,' and it will obey you.'"*

**Luke 17:19**

*"Then he said to him, 'Rise and go; your faith has made you well.'"*

**Luke 18:8**

*"I tell you, he will see that they get justice, and quickly. However, when the Son of Man comes, will he find faith on the earth?"*

**Luke 18:42**

*"Jesus said to him, 'Receive your sight; your faith has healed you.'"*

### Luke 22:32

"But I have prayed for you, Simon, that your faith may not fail. And when you have turned back, strengthen your brothers."

### Acts 3:16

"By faith in the name of Jesus, this man whom you see and know was made strong. It is Jesus' name and the faith that comes through him that has given this complete healing to him, as you can all see."

### Acts 6:5

"This proposal pleased the whole group. They chose Stephen, a man full of faith and of the Holy Spirit; also Philip, Procorus, Nicanor, Timon, Parmenas, and Nicolas from Antioch, a convert to Judaism."

### Acts 6:7

"So the word of God spread. The number of disciples in Jerusalem increased rapidly, and a large number of priests became obedient to the faith."

### Acts 6:8

"And Stephen, full of faith and power, did great wonders and signs among the people." (NKJV)

### Acts 11:24

"He was a good man, full of the Holy Spirit and faith, and a great number of people were brought to the Lord."

### Acts 14:9

"He listened to Paul as he was speaking. Paul looked directly at him, saw that he had faith to be healed."

### Romans 1:8

"First, I thank my God through Jesus Christ for all of you, because your faith is being reported all over the world."

**Romans 1:12**

*"That is, that you and I may be mutually encouraged by each other's faith."*

**Romans 4:16**

*"Therefore, the promise comes by faith, so that it may be by grace and may be guaranteed to all Abraham's offspring—not only to those who are of the law but also to those who are of the faith of Abraham. He is the father of us all."*

**Romans 4:19**

*"Without weakening in his faith, he faced the fact that his body was as good as dead—since he was about a hundred years old—and that Sarah's womb was also dead."*

**Romans 4:20**

*"Yet he did not waver through unbelief regarding the promise of God, but was strengthened in his faith and gave glory to God."*

**Romans 10:8**

*"But what does it say? "The word is near you; it is in your mouth and in your heart," that is, the word of faith we are proclaiming."*

**Romans 10:17**

*"Consequently, faith comes from hearing the message, and the message is heard through the word of Christ."*

**Romans 11:20**

*"Granted. But they were broken off because of unbelief, and you stand by faith. Do not be arrogant, but be afraid."*

**1 Corinthians 2:5**

*"So that your faith might not rest on men's wisdom, but on God's power."*

### I Corinthians 13:2

*"If I have the gift of prophecy and can fathom all myster- ies and all knowledge, and if I have a faith that can move mountains, but have not love, I am nothing."*

### I Corinthians 13:13

*"And now these three remain: faith, hope and love. But the greatest of these is love."*

### 2 Corinthians 1:24

*"Not that we lord it over your faith, but we work with you for your joy, because it is by faith you stand firm."*

### 2 Corinthians 4:13

*"It is written: 'I believed; therefore I have spoken.' With that same spirit of faith we also believe and therefore speak."*

### 2 Corinthians 5:7

*"We live by faith, not by sight."*

### 2 Corinthian 8:7

*"But just as you excel in everything—in faith, in speech, in knowledge, in complete earnestness and in your love for us—see that you also excel in this grace of giving."*

### 2 Corinthians 10:15

*"Neither do we go beyond our limits by boasting of work done by others. Our hope is that, as your faith continues to grow, our area of activity among you will greatly expand,"*

### Galatians 2:20

*"I have been crucified with Christ and I no longer live, but Christ lives in me. The life I live in the body, I live by faith in the Son of God, who loved me and gave himself for me."*

### Galatians 3:9

*"So those who have faith are blessed along with Abraham, the man of faith."*

### Galatians 3:11

*"Clearly no one is justified before God by the law, because, 'The righteous will live by faith.'"*

### Galatians 3:14

*"He redeemed us in order that the blessing given to Abraham might come to the Gentiles through Christ Jesus, so that by faith we might receive the promise of the Spirit."*

### Galatians 3:22

*"But the Scripture declares that the whole world is a prisoner of sin, so that what was promised, being given through faith in Jesus Christ, might be given to those who believe."*

### Galatians 5:5

*"But by faith we eagerly await through the Spirit the righteousness for which we hope."*

### Ephesians 3:12

*"In him and through faith in him we may approach God with freedom and confidence."*

### Ephesians 6:16

*"In addition to all this, take up the shield of faith, with which you can extinguish all the flaming arrows of the evil one."*

### Colossians 1:23

*"If you continue in your faith, established and firm, not moved from the hope held out in the gospel. This is the gospel that you heard and that has been proclaimed to every creature under heaven, and of which I, Paul, have become a servant."*

### Colossians 2:5

*"For though I am absent from you in body, I am present with you in spirit and delight to see how orderly you are and how firm your faith in Christ is."*

**Colossians 2:7**

*"Rooted and built up in him, strengthened in the faith as you were taught, and overflowing with thankfulness."*

**1 Thessalonians 3:10**

*"Night and day we pray most earnestly that we may see you again and supply what is lacking in your faith."*

**1 Thessalonians 5:8**

*"But since we belong to the day, let us be self-controlled, putting on faith and love as a breastplate, and the hope of salvation as a helmet."*

**2 Thessalonians 1:3**

*"We ought always to thank God for you, brothers, and rightly so, because your faith is growing more and more, and the love every one of you has for each other is increasing."*

**2 Thessalonians 1:11**

*"With this in mind, we constantly pray for you, that our God may count you worthy of his calling, and that by his power he may fulfill every good purpose of yours and every act prompted by your faith."*

**1 Timothy 6:11**

*"But you, man of God, flee from all this, and pursue righteousness, godliness, faith, love, endurance and gentleness."*

**1 Timothy 6:12**

*"Fight the good fight of the faith. Take hold of the eternal life to which you were called when you made your good confession in the presence of many witnesses."*

**Hebrews 11:1**

*"Now faith is being sure of what we hope for and certain of what we do not see."*

### Hebrews 11:3

*"By faith we understand that the universe was formed at God's command, so that what is seen was not made out of what was visible."*

### Hebrews 11:4

*"By faith Abel offered God a better sacrifice than Cain did. By faith he was commended as a righteous man, when God spoke well of his offerings. And by faith he still speaks, even though he is dead."*

### Hebrews 11:5

*"By faith Enoch was taken from this life, so that he did not experience death; he could not be found, because God had taken him away. For before he was taken, he was commended as one who pleased God."*

### Hebrews 11:6

*"And without faith it is impossible to please God, because anyone who comes to him must believe that he exists and that he rewards those who earnestly seek him."*

### Hebrews 11:7

*"By faith Noah, when warned about things not yet seen, in holy fear built an ark to save his family. By his faith he condemned the world and became heir of the righteousness that comes by faith."*

### Hebrews 11:8

*"By faith Abraham, when called to go to a place he would later receive as his inheritance, obeyed and went, even though he did not know where he was going."*

### Hebrews 11:9

*"By faith he made his home in the promised land like a stranger in a foreign country; he lived in tents, as did Isaac and Jacob, who were heirs with him of the same promise."*

**Hebrews 11:11**

"By faith Abraham, even though he was past age—and Sarah herself was barren—was enabled to become a father because he considered him faithful who had made the promise."

**Hebrews 11:13**

"All these people were still living by faith when they died. They did not receive the things promised; they only saw them and welcomed them from a distance. And they admitted that they were aliens and strangers on earth."

**Hebrews 11:17**

"By faith Abraham, when God tested him, offered Isaac as a sacrifice. He who had received the promises was about to sacrifice his one and only son."

**Hebrews 11:20**

"By faith Isaac blessed Jacob and Esau in regard to their future."

**Hebrews 11:21**

"By faith Jacob, when he was dying, blessed each of Joseph's sons, and worshiped as he leaned on the top of his staff."

**Hebrews 11:22**

"By faith Joseph, when his end was near, spoke about the exodus of the Israelites from Egypt and gave instructions about his bones."

**Hebrews 11:23**

"By faith Moses' parents hid him for three months after he was born, because they saw he was no ordinary child, and they were not afraid of the king's edict."

**Hebrews 11:24**

"By faith Moses, when he had grown up, refused to be known as the son of Pharaoh's daughter."

**Hebrews 11:27**

"By faith he left Egypt, not fearing the king's anger; he persevered because he saw him who is invisible."

**Hebrews 11:28**

"By faith he kept the Passover and the sprinkling of blood, so that the destroyer of the firstborn would not touch the firstborn of Israel."

**Hebrews 11:29**

"By faith the people passed through the Red Sea as on dry land; but when the Egyptians tried to do so, they were drowned."

**Hebrews 11:30**

"By faith the walls of Jericho fell, after the people had marched around them for seven days."

**Hebrews 11:31**

"By faith the prostitute Rahab, because she welcomed the spies, was not killed with those who were disobedient."

**Hebrews 11:33**

"Who through faith conquered kingdoms, administered justice, and gained what was promised; who shut the mouths of lions."

**Hebrews 11:39**

"These were all commended for their faith, yet none of them received what had been promised."

**Hebrews 12:2**

"Let us fix our eyes on Jesus, the author and perfecter of our faith, who for the joy set before him endured the cross, scorning its shame, and sat down at the right hand of the throne of God."

**Hebrews 13:7**

*"Remember your leaders, who spoke the word of God to you. Consider the outcome of their way of life and imitate their faith."*

**James 1:3**

*"Because you know that the testing of your faith develops perseverance."*

**James 1:6**

*"But when he asks, he must believe and not doubt, because he who doubts is like a wave of the sea, blown and tossed by the wind."*

**James 2:5**

*"Listen, my dear brothers: Has not God chosen those who are poor in the eyes of the world to be rich in faith and to inherit the kingdom he promised those who love him?"*

**James 2:14**

*"What good is it, my brothers, if a man claims to have faith but has no deeds? Can such faith save him?"*

**James 2:17**

*"In the same way, faith by itself, if it is not accompanied by action, is dead."*

**James 2:18**

*"But someone will say, "You have faith; I have deeds." Show me your faith without deeds, and I will show you my faith by what I do."*

**James 2:20**

*"You foolish man, do you want evidence that faith without deeds is useless?"*

**James 2:22**

*"You see that his faith and his actions were working together, and his faith was made complete by what he did."*

**James 2:24**

"You see that a person is justified by what he does and not by faith alone."

**James 2:26**

"As the body without the spirit is dead, so faith without deeds is dead."

**James 5:15**

"And the prayer offered in faith will make the sick person well; the Lord will raise him up. If he has sinned, he will be forgiven."

**1 Peter 1:5**

"Who through faith are shielded by God's power until the coming of the salvation that is ready to be revealed in the last time."

**1 Peter 1:7**

"These have come so that your faith—of greater worth than gold, which perishes even though refined by fire—may be proved genuine and may result in praise, glory and honor when Jesus Christ is revealed."

**1 Peter 1:21**

"Through him you believe in God, who raised him from the dead and glorified him, and so your faith and hope are in God."

**1 John 5:4**

"For everyone born of God overcomes the world. This is the victory that has overcome the world, even our faith."

**Revelation 2:19**

"I know your deeds, your love and faith, your service and perseverance, and that you are now doing more than you did at first."

## Summary

So faith is not just some mind-set or intangible thing. It is an act. Much like grace. Grace is more than just unmerited favor, or the fact that we have received something from God that we do not deserve. Grace is God's operational activity in our daily lives. All the heroes of faith recorded in the eleventh chapter of Hebrews are said to have done something that gave evidence of their faith.

When we are truly activating our God given faith, we will act upon it. If you claim a promise of God, you may not know the exact moment the manifestation will occur, but it always comes as you are acting in agreement with your confession of faith in God's Word. It will never come in the midst of doubt or failure to act on your faith.

# Source Material

21 Unbreakable Laws of Success, Max Anders, Thomas Nelson, 1996

A Christian Guide to Prosperity; Fries & Taylor, California: Communications Research, 1984

A Look At Stewardship, Word Aflame Publications, 2001

American Savings Education Council (http://www.asec.org)

Anointed For Business, Ed Silvoso, Regal, 2002

Avoiding Common Financial Mistakes, Ron Blue, Navpress, 1991

Baker Encyclopedia of the Bible; Walter Elwell, Michigan: Baker Book House, 1988

Becoming The Best, Barry Popplewell, England: Gower Publishing Company Limited, 1988

Business Proverbs, Steve Marr, Fleming H. Revell, 2001

Cheapskate Monthly, Mary Hunt

Commentary on the Old Testament; Keil-Delitzsch, Michigan: Eerdmans Publishing, 1986

Crown Financial Ministries, various publications

Customers As Partners, Chip Bell, Texas: Berrett-Koehler Publishers, 1994

Cut Your Bills in Half; Pennsylvania: Rodale Press, Inc., 1989

Debt-Free Living, Larry Burkett, Dimensions, 2001

Die Broke, Stephen M. Pollan & Mark Levine, HarperBusiness, 1997

Double Your Profits, Bob Fifer, Virginia: Lincoln Hall Press, 1993

Eerdmans' Handbook to the Bible, Michigan: William B. Eerdmans Publishing Company, 1987

Eight Steps to Seven Figures, Charles B. Carlson, Double Day, 2000

Everyday Life in Bible Times; Washington DC: National Geographic Society, 1967

Financial Dominion, Norvel Hayes, Harrison House, 1986

Financial Freedom, Larry Burkett, Moody Press, 1991

Financial Freedom, Patrick Clements, VMI Publishers, 2003

Financial Peace, Dave Ramsey, Viking Press, 2003

Financial Self-Defense; Charles Givens, New York: Simon And Schuster, 1990

Flood Stage, Oral Roberts, 1981

Generous Living, Ron Blue, Zondervan, 1997

Get It All Done, Tony and Robbie Fanning, New York:Pennsylvania: Chilton Book, 1979

Getting Out of Debt, Howard Dayton, Tyndale House, 1986

Getting Out of Debt, Mary Stephenson, Fact Sheet 436, University of Maryland Cooperative Extension Service, 1988

Giving and Tithing, Larry Burkett, Moody Press, 1991

God's Plan For Giving, John MacArthur, Jr., Moody Press, 1985

God's Will is Prosperity, Gloria Copeland, Harrison House, 1978

Great People of the Bible and How They Lived; New York: Reader's Digest, 1974

How Others Can Help You Get Out of Debt; Esther M. Maddux, Circular 759-3,

How To Make A Business Plan That Works, Henderson, North Island Sound Limited, 1989

How To Manage Your Money, Larry Burkett, Moody Press, 1999

How to Personally Profit From the Laws of Success, Sterling Sill, NIFP, Inc., 1978

How to Plan for Your Retirement; New York: Corrigan & Kaufman, Longmeadow Press, 1985

Is God Your Source?, Oral Roberts, 1992

It's Not Luck, Eliyahu Goldratt, Great Barrington, MA: The North River Press, 1994

Jesus CEO, Laurie Beth Jones, Hyperion, 1995

John Avanzini Answers Your Questions About Biblical Economics, Harrison House, 1992

Living on Less and Liking It More, Maxine Hancock, Chicago, Illinois: Moody Press, 1976

Making It Happen; Charles Conn, New Jersey: Fleming H. Revell Company, 1981

Master Your Money Or It Will Master You, Arlo E. Moehlenpah, Doing Good Ministries, 1999

Master Your Money; Ron Blue, Tennessee: Thomas Nelson, Inc. 1986

Miracle of Seed Faith, Oral Roberts, 1970

Mississippi State University Extension Service

Money, Possessions, and Eternity, Randy Alcorn, Tyndale House, 2003

More Than Enough, David Ramsey, Penguin Putnam Inc, 2002

Moving the Hand of God, John Avanzini, Harrison House, 1990

Multiplication, Tommy Barnett, Creation House, 1997

NebFacts, Nebraska Cooperative Extension

New York Post

One Up On Wall Street; New York: Peter Lynch, Simon And Schuster, 1989

Personal Finances, Larry Burkett, Moody Press, 1991

Portable MBA in Finance and Accounting; Livingstone, Canada: John Wiley & Sons, Inc., 1992

Principle-Centered Leadership, Stephen R. Covey, New York: Summit Books, 1991

Principles of Financial Management, Kolb & DeMong, Texas: Business Publications, Inc., 1988

Rapid Debt Reduction Strategies, John Avanzini, HIS Publishing, 1990

Real Wealth, Wade Cook, Arizona: Regency Books, 1985

See You At The Top, Zig Ziglar, Louisianna: Pelican Publishing Company, 1977

Seed-Faith Commentary on the Holy Bible, Oral Roberts, Pinoak Publications, 1975

Sharkproof, Harvey Mackay, New York: HarperCollins Publishers, 1993

Smart Money, Ken and Daria Dolan, New York: Random House, Inc., 1988

Strong's Concordance, Tennessee: Crusade Bible Publishers, Inc.,

Success by Design, Peter Hirsch, Bethany House, 2002

Success is the Quality of your Journey, Jennifer James, New York: Newmarket Press, 1983

Swim with the Sharks Without Being Eaten Alive, Harvey Mackay, William Morrow , 1988

The Almighty and the Dollar; Jim McKeever, Oregon: Omega Publications, 1981

The Challenge, Robert Allen, New York: Simon And Schuster, 1987

The Family Financial Workbook, Larry Burkett, Moody Press, 2002

The Management Methods of Jesus, Bob Briner, Thomas Nelson, 1996

The Millionaire Next Door, Thomas Stanley & William Danko, Pocket Books, 1996

The Money Book for Kids, Nancy Burgeson, Troll Associates,1992

The Money Book for King's Kids; Harold E. Hill, New Jersey: Fleming H. Revell Company, 1984

The Seven Habits of Highly Effective People, Stephen Covey, New York: Simon And Schuster, 1989

The Wealthy Barber, David Chilton, California: Prima Publishing, 1991

Theological Wordbook of the Old Testament, Chicago, Illinois: Moody Press, 1981

Treasury of Courage and Confidence, Norman Vincent Peale, New York: Doubleday & Co., 1970

True Prosperity, Dick Iverson, Bible Temple Publishing, 1993

Trust God For Your Finances, Jack Hartman, Lamplight Publications, 1983

University of Georgia Cooperative Extension Service, 1985

Virginia Cooperative Extension

Webster's Unabridged Dictionary, Dorset & Baber, 1983

What Is an Entrepreneur; David Robinson, MA: Kogan Page Limited, 1990

Word Meanings in the New Testament, Ralph Earle, Michigan: Baker Book House, 1986

Word Pictures in the New Testament; Robertson, Michigan: Baker Book House, 1930

Word Studies in the New Testament; Vincent, New York: Charles Scribner's Sons, 1914

Worth

You Can Be Financially Free, George Fooshee, Jr., 1976, Fleming H. Revell Company.

Your Key to God's Bank, Rex Humbard, 1977

Your Money Counts, Howard, Dayton, Tyndale House, 1997

Your Money Management, MaryAnn Paynter, Circular 1271, University of Illinois Cooperative Extension Service, 1987.

Your Money Matters, Malcolm MacGregor, Bethany Fellowship, Inc., 1977

Your Road to Recovery, Oral Roberts, Oliver Nelson, 1986

## Comments On Sources

Over the years I have collected bits and pieces of interesting material, written notes on sermons I've heard, jotted down comments on financial articles I've read, and gathered a lot of great information. It is unfortunate that I didn't record the sources of all of these notes in my earlier years.  I gratefully extend my appreciation to the many writers, authors, teachers and pastors from whose articles and sermons I have gleaned much insight.

*Rich Brott*

# Online Resources

American Savings Education Council (http://www.asec.org)

Bloomberg.com (http://www.bloomberg.com)

Bureau of the Public Debt Online (http://www.publicdebt.treas.gov)

BusinessWeek (http://www.businessweek.com)

Charles Schwab & Co., Inc. (http://www.schwab.com)

Consumer Federation of America (http://www.consumerfed.org)

Debt Advice.org (http://www.debtadvice.org)

Federal Reserve System  (http://www.federalreserve.gov)

Fidelity Investments (http://www.fidelity.com)

Financial Planning Association (http://www.fpanet.org)

Forbes (www.forbes.com)

Fortune Magazine (http://www.fortune.com)

Generous Giving (http://www.generousgiving.org/)

Investing for Your Future (http://www.investing.rutgers.edu)

Kiplinger Magazine (http://www.kiplinger.com/)

Money Magazine (http://money.cnn.com)

MorningStar (http://www.morningstar.com)

MSN Money (http://moneycentral.msn.com)

Muriel Siebert (http://www.siebertnet.com)

National Center on Education and the Economy (http://www.ncee.org)

National Foundation for Credit Counseling (http://www.nfcc.org)

Quicken (http://www.quicken.com)

Smart Money (http://www.smartmoney.com)

Social Security Online (http://www.ssa.gov)

Standard & Poor's (http://www2.standardandpoors.com)

The Dollar Stretcher, Gary Foreman, (http://www.stretcher.com)

The Vanguard Group (http://flagship.vanguard.com)

U.S. Securities and Exchange Commission (http://www.sec.gov)

Yahoo! Finance (http://finance.yahoo.com)

# *Magazine Resources*

Business Week
Consumer Reports
Forbes
Kiplinger's Personal Finance
Money
Smart Money
US News and World Report

# Newspaper Resources

Barrons
Investors Business Daily
USA Today
Wall Street Journal
Washington Times

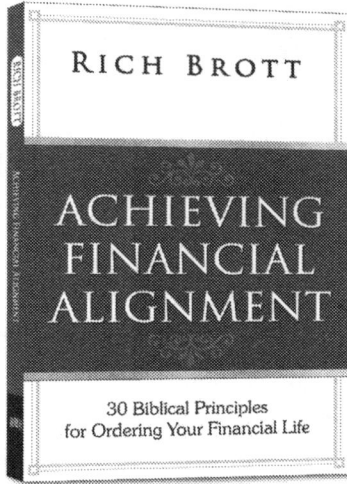

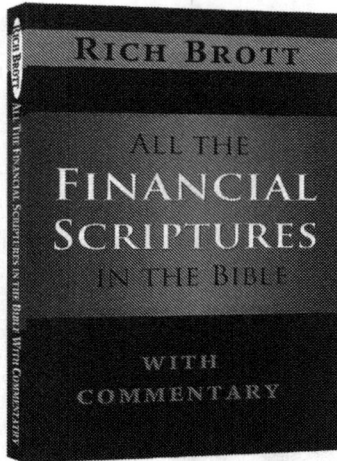

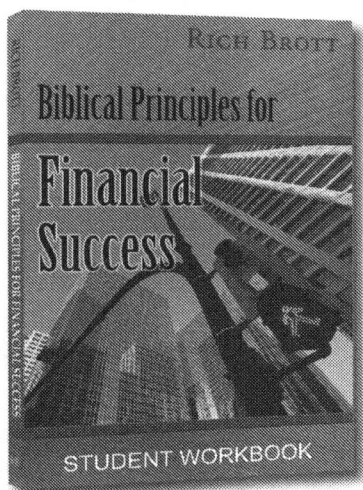

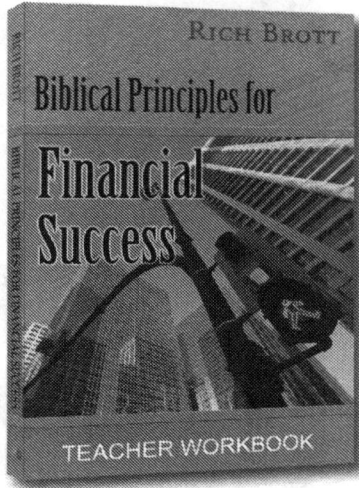

## Biblical Principles for
## Financial Success

*Teacher Workbook*

By Rich Brott

7.5" x 9.25", 228 pages
ISBN 1-60185-015-8
ISBN (EAN) 978-1-60185-015-7

a b c
Book Publishing

*Order online at:*
www.RichBrott.com
www.amazon.com
www.barnesandnoble.com
www.booksamillion.com
www.citychristianpublishing.com
www.bordersstores.com

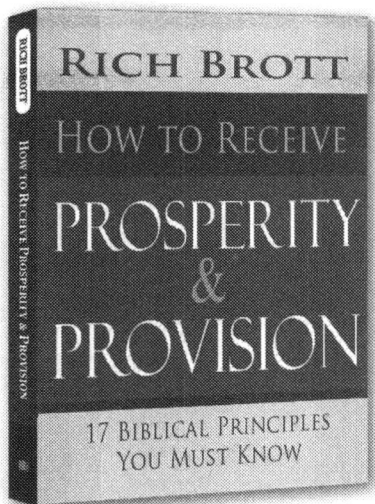